No Bad Days...
I Can Eat This Pizza:

JOURNEYS WITH A SOCIAL WORKER

MATTHEW A. ELDRIDGE

Fulton Books
Meadville, PA

Published by Fulton Books 2022

ISBN 978-1-64952-068-5 (paperback)
ISBN 978-1-64952-069-2 (digital)

Printed in the United States of America

Contents

Preface

I never saw the day I would be a social worker. My training as an undergraduate was putting me on the path toward being a policy researcher, working for a think tank, and/or going into Culinary Arts as a chef and/or manager. However, some accidents happen in the most amazing ways. When I graduated in 2005 with my undergraduate degrees, I was picked to open a Marriott Hotel-franchised property as the breakfast chef and server, and in this role, I also did catering and special events.

Due to hostilities in the workplace, I left and became a server and backup chef for another company, and that led to being selected as a dietary chef for an Assisted Living. Due to needing to pick up a few extra hours, I accepted a part-time job as an Activities Director for a senior/adult foster home—that allowed when the Resident Manager position came open, I was able to transition into that role. There is so much more I could write about my experiences managing a foster home, but I will spare that. However, there are things learned that I will share as we go through the *Journeys with a Social Worker*.

There is something all members of any social worker profession must understand: documentation is your friend. Yes, it can be a pain, takes time, and may seem unnecessary, yet when it comes time to need it, you want it there and not have to create it. In fact, it would be unethical to create the documentation to match what you need. Rather, if you are doing your documentation correctly, doing your job judiciously, you will not have to worry about documentation being a problem supporting what you need. Why do I write that? As a Resident Manager, I had already given my notice that I was leaving. The final week of my resignation, a series of narcotics and other non-narcotics that I had kept a tally on were missing: They were there Friday when I went off shift for the weekend, and when I came back on Monday morning, they had been missing.

This writer had reported to the provider/owner of the foster home, called the pharmacy to let them know early requests for narcotics would be made, and was instructed to contact the doctors. The provider failed to do any reporting—I had been in contact with a contract nurse for the state about the missing meds, and she instructed I had until 8:00 a.m. the next morning to report to DHS, or I would have my license investigated. In short, had I not created a narcotics records for this facility, there would be no way to prove (1) that the meds were accounted for and (2) that they were missing specifically during a period that this writer was out of commission.

In my final shift, I had written my progress notes. I had a funny feeling that things could be done wrong or my records altered after leaving; therefore, I wrote the final reports in blue ink (at that time, we did handwritten notes, and that is not likely the same now for audiences reading) and reported in my notes that if these notes are in any other color than blue, it means they have been altered and copied and changed from what was written by myself.

There is a saying in social services: "Cover Your Ass." And you bet we in social work do this because there are civil and criminal penalties to doing things wrong in our profession. Let me challenge you. If you are not doing this to ensure that you are protected, you are taking a risk that might sink you. That said, if you are doing things in social services that are not ethical and/or illegal, it might take time, but circumstances will catch up. Most of all, documentation takes time, but without taking that time, you are doing an injustice to your client(s), agency, and yourself. Regardless if you are a volunteer social worker, intern, and/or a paid employee, the standards apply across the board. The responsibilities do not change, and failure to not know the laws around what you are doing is just as risky as driving a car without a license. Like driving a car, you may get a license for a lifetime, yet that does not mean you are released from the responsibility of knowing the updated laws and procedures in your profession. On another note, the license you hold, the body that credentials you, all those might have greater standards than the generally accepted legal standards—you might be okay legally, but you can be in trouble with those specific boards.

If you are working for a company that has satellite branches in other states, ensure that you know what the rules are for each State because you will be bound by them if working in those geographic areas. If you have read so far, I welcome you to now join me as I bring you through different journeys experienced as a Qualified Mental Health Associate (QMHA), Navigator, provider of geriatrics care, and advocate for my late paternal Grandmother and Father. As clients have not signed releases, names and places have been changed to protect them and, in reality, myself for reasons discussed above. The best part of this read is, the stories will never end once published because each client will provide a unique opportunity.

Please understand, each client is *unique*; their situation is not like any other. Yes, circumstances might be the same as what you have encountered; however, the situation is specific to that human/client. If treating a couple, family, etc., attempt to look through a single lens and attempt to not cast a wide blanket of understanding. That said, do attempt to apply what you learned from a previous case experience.

I want to leave you all with one thing before we start this journey: be willing to be vulnerable! I am bipolar, had my break in 2007, got help, and have been able to manage my mental health by abiding my treatment, and this has allowed me to have compassion and understanding toward my clients. I have also been in recovery for alcohol and drug use since 2005, and this allows me to understand dual diagnosis in ways that go beyond an academic approach. I am open with clients. My issues with alcohol and drugs was solved before having kids and/or getting married. I do not share all this immediately with clients and sometimes not with others. When possible, be willing to engage with your clients if you have means of relating to them. Speaking of relating, regardless of your employment restrictions, do not add clients (if you are a volunteer in a church or something, that might be different) to your social media platforms. We can be friendly toward them, yet we do not want to create a perception that we are friends. If you are honest with yourself, you will understand that there is a power differential that does exist, and keeping good boundaries will help your professional life—it will in fact cover your ass!

Buckle up, enjoy the ride, and most of all, keep an open mind. We will discuss issues of gender, sexuality, abuse, manipulation, violence, differences of religion, politics, and any social identification issue you can think of. This is their life, not yours. It's my journey through helping clients and advocating for my Grandma and Father, and if you are offended and cannot separate your dogmas, I can assure you, you are not ready for social services. Being in social services means that you put your own biases aside and focus on the person needing your help. Most of all, help out of compassion or move over for someone to help.

A final note before we start this journey: this is not meant to be an academic presentation. I will use my academic understanding of concepts learned and my practical backgrounds. You will not find citations (instead, you will be asked to engage in your own research/nerding) because this is more of a biography of clients' journeys and my own journey advocating and parenting my disabled Father and late Grandma. I promise to attempt to be professional in my presentation, but I promise you may be offended. I fundamentally fight against academic dishonesty and plagiarism, believe in client confidentiality, and believe standards of decency.

What you will notice as you read this exposé is, I was groomed to be a social worker and never understood it. My volunteer work, the compassion I have toward humans, my education, and my life experiences were calling me to this field. Some accidents will ruin your life, but this accident was meant to be and has influenced the lives of countless. My experiences as a Sunday School Teacher, Coach, and working in geriatrics, in sales, and in the office have all paved the way. My hope for you is, do not let your education or lack of education, social work experience or lack thereof disqualify you—it is about compassion and desire and remaining coachable.

As you can tell, my résumé is diverse. It contains culinary arts, marketing, sales, nearly every aspect of geriatrics, mental health, office work, and resource identification. I have a strong record of volunteer work and youth engagement (Sunday School Teacher and Speech and Debate Coach), and I hope you understand that your journey into social work, geriatrics, and/or resource identification might also happen by accident. The goal of this book is to empower you.

Introduction

A title should mean something. As a social worker, I have gained titles, including Certified QMHA and Navigator. I am also a Speech and Debate Coach/Mentor. I am also a licensed Senior and Adult Foster Care Resident Manager and licensed in Developmental Disabilities Foster Care. I have two undergraduate BS degrees, a minor in Women's Studies, and an MBA with focus in Management, but these education qualities are only tools to accomplish my work as a social worker. If you believe education qualifies you for social work, this book will answer why that is not true; your education should help you become a well-rounded person and be used to have an impact on your clients and the agency that puts you in touch with these clients.

What about the titles of presentations? This presentation's title captures two statements of two different clients whose lives radically changed because of the impact this social worker and many others had on them. You see, my client Richard, when he got sober, explained, "My worst day sober is better than my best day high." And then he concluded "No Bad Days" as his new motto. Then another client, Kim, was given some money by coworkers after work to buy a pizza. Kim explained that for the past three years, this would be her first time buying a pizza that she would not have to share and justify eating it, and out of nowhere, she reports, "I Can Eat This Pizza." That influenced my writings today because if you can understand and come to a conclusion that there are no bad days and that this person gained freedom to eat something as simple as pizza as life-changing realities for these clients, you will either be energized to applaud them (even having never met them) or be ready to help someone else have no bad days and empower them to eat their pizza too.

I want to challenge anyone who wants to enter social work to understand the trauma brain. Should this statement have you baffled, please stop, look it up, gain an understanding, then proceed with reading. If this idea is not new to you, ask yourself, What does the trauma brain look like from one client to another, from one sex to another, from one sexual orientation to another? And then I will challenge you again, Do you understand your clients ACEs? If you have never heard of ACEs, again, please stop, look up Adverse Childhood Experiences, and understand what these are and how to talk to your clients about them because this will really help you. No, you do not have to complete an ACEs with every client; rather, be prepared to know it, understand it, and help them understand how those are affecting them and others.

In my years of social work, I have worked in Community Mental Health, did a Practicum for a Community Organization, worked in a Skilled Nursing Home as a nonlicensed Social Services Director, and worked as a contracted service provider for Navigator Services. I have used my talents to help my students as a coach, have listened to other coaches to gain understanding of the ins/outs of working with youth, and have also been a Personal Support Worker (PWS) for children with developmental disabilities. Let me challenge you. Learn different aspects of social work; do not get comfortable with just one area. Work on an interdisciplinary team to enhance your interactions. Of all, leave your personal biases in your vehicle, the parking lot—in other words, do not bring them into your office. Even if you are working for yourself, you are working for the greater good—the client asking for your help. Let me warn you, if you work harder than the client, you will burn out, get frustrated, and therefore, tell your clients what you need from them. Get some buy-in, and make it a team effort. I promise, not often will you get immediate buy-in from your clients; at some point, you must expect it for yours and their good.

Both of the clients referenced in this presentation's title are shocking: they closed their services with this writer fully achieved and their lives changed. It is on them to stay sober and such, but all the tools are there, and their outcomes were not expected to the degree that they are. Richard had significant disabilities; it was looking like "Richard" would not be able to regain custody of his child at the time reunification happened; this all happened because when he got sober, he figured out that this writer as going to advocate for him, so he got on board. Caution: if your client(s) boards the train and you are not ready to go, there will be a problem. Always be ready to engage once they say YES. In fact, failure to engage right then may be the thing that ruins any attempt to get them to buy in, in the future and/or get them to accomplish what is necessary. I promise you, your clients will not wait for their social worker to board the train.

When looking at Kim's story, she was living under a bridge during the cold of winter, had been for several months, and did not believe there was hope or that she could do better. On the streets, Kim had come into an abusive relationship. Kim was convinced that she loved this person (no doubt that she did love the perpetrator), but Kim was not being loved in return. Many conversations happened with her about why she needs to love herself more than believing that is the best she can do. Long story short, Kim got approved for domestic violence crisis shelter and moved in, and less than thirty days later, she found a job, took medications, got medical care needed, found a room for rent, and came to a conclusion, "I can eat this pizza." Can I challenge you? The next time you spend money on a carryout pizza, think about the fact that you are doing this without thought. Kim, as a result of combination of life choices and circumstances, would have to share, ask permission, or believe it would not be her pizza even though it was bought for her. Please never think of something as simple as pizza the same again because there are battered victims who would dream of having that same pizza but know it is not there's to be had any more than their bodies.

As alluded in the previous statement, some of the clients whom I have come across have sold their dignity and bodies for survival. If you have a home (even a tiny house), heat, food, and a lover who is safe with you, do not take these things for granted. This social worker has worked with countless clients who have sold their dignity and sexual expression and have criminal records all in the name of self-preservation. If this is all too much to handle for you, I appreciate your honesty and do not believe social work is for you, but if this outrages you to make a difference, harness that negative energy in a positive way and get involved. Life is sacred; dignity is precious. As a social worker, you can make a sacred and dignified difference in your clients' lives, and most social workers (teachers and coaches included) will never likely know how much of a difference they have made in their clients' and/or students' lives. This writer is fortunate to have seen some of the differences made, and it is because of that that I want to bring my audience on a journey. This journey is isolated to the state of Oregon, USA; however, the takeaways are universal if applied.

Each of the chapters covered in the presentation are purposeful and represent my scope of experience. I do not believe they will apply to every social worker and/or every experience. To believe that is arrogance, and social workers should not be arrogant. Confident? Yes. We should know what are doing and know that we can help our clients, but what you do with one client is not always going to be archetypal to the next client. Please do not believe what works for one member of the family will also work for another member of that family. Humans are unique; they are their own beings, and to consider them any different is abusive and wrong! For those who write Care Plans and/or Treatment Plans, make them specific, purposeful, and measurable to your client. A template can be used, but do not let that template marginalize your client.

This presentation is written not for an audience who has been doing social work forever—although you may find something of value—but rather for the person who wants to enter our field, who wants to advance in the industry, who is starting school and/or about to graduate, the person in recovery who wants to help. This will help a Program Manager and/or Supervisor train their social workers on how to better identify their biases and become resource nerds. Maybe you want to be a volunteer and/or want to create a program through your church or civic group but need some direction. I hope this will be of value. Please remember, this is my social worker (and geriatrics) journey, and your journey may not look the same, but the mission and mandate of compassion will likely be the same.

I ask that you don't cherry-pick chapters; the content builds chapter to chapter, and you will lose valuable understanding if you do not read each chapter. This is not a hard-to-read academic writing because I am not interested in that. I am interested in you gaining skills and seeing humanity from a perspective you may not have seen. It is important to understand that every story told here is real; there is nothing fictional about my writing. The examples have either been lived by work in geriatrics, social work, and academia or witnessed as lived out by other social workers that I have been a cohort with or through my experiences advocating for my family. Frequently, I am going to ask my readers to consider your biases. I am not asking you to change your worldview. In order to be an effective dynamic social worker, your ability to love and respect people and their circumstances is paramount. Welcome aboard and thanks for boarding the biographical journey.

ROIs Are Critical

As discussed earlier, paperwork and social work are not possible without each other. Part of the paperwork is doing proper and legal ROIs. First, do you know what an ROI is? Officially, it stands for Release of Information, but unofficially, it is your key to unlocking many doors. But like a residence, there are locks on the door and sometimes a dead bolt, and not always the same key opens both locks. Confused? Let's dive in.

Each agency, organization, and/or program should have an ROI approved by your Compliance Officer(s). To be legal, exact name, DOB, signature, date, and purpose must be filled out. But that is not all. If you are dealing with mental health, HIV, Alcohol/Drugs, genetics, etc., in order to release this information, it must further be initialed by the client and/or their Legal Guardian. If your client initials that you can talk about Urine Analysis but fails to initial the Alcohol/Drug portion, you MAY NOT talk about their A&D UAs. In fact, most of us in social services and just being a consumer of health care services, maybe use of social services or general hospital care, have likely been exposed to the idea of HIPAA or what HIPAA protections are meant to secure your protected information. There is an advanced thing, 42 CFR Part 2, that was passed many years before HIPAA that is specific to Alcohol and Drug information. Being on the wrong side of HIPAA and/or 42 CFR Part 2 can financially, ethically, and professionally hurt you, your clients, and even your employer.

Please do not assume! If someone calls you, e-mails you, wants information from you, claims to have an ROI and your agency does not have one on file, ASK FOR IT. Seeing is BELIEVING because WITHOUT SEEING, you should NOT BELIEVE it exists. Yes, it may exist, but what is the purpose of the ROI? If the client did not specify the specific purpose of what information to be released, to whom/what/why, you should ignore the request. In my own journey of advocating and now being the Legal Guardian of my Father, I have had to sign ROIs for his acute care needs. I have ensured that the hospital he is at has an ROI and, when possible, will ensure the organization being requested to share information has a copy. There is such a thing as Coordination of Care; however, this needs to be spoken with your Compliance Officer to ensure that if you are releasing information on the basis of Coordination of Care, you are following the rules that govern it. This is too messy for me to dive into and will likely change from situation to situation; therefore, I am empowering you to understand it exists but use caution when engaging with this kind of release of PHI.

Not long ago, I had entered a community housing provider asking specific questions about a client. I had an ROI that allowed me to engage in these questions. The social worker asked, "Do you have an ROI for said client?" She would not even acknowledge the client's name, but once I produced my ROI, we engaged in a formal and productive conversation. Professionally and ethically, I had a right to ask about my client; the other social worker was absolutely correct in demanding to see my ROI. In the future, when I engage with a community provider about a mutual client, I will soften their approach by giving them a copy of my client's ROI immediately. This experience affected me in a positive way because it identified how I can be a more efficient and professional social worker. I consider myself a seasoned social worker, and that moment taught me something—be open to learning as a social worker.

Perhaps you struggle with this this next problem: "But I might hurt someone's feelings if I do not answer their questions." Seriously, hurt feelings in social work are going to happen, but hurt feelings do not cost you ethic inquiry and financial penalties. If you have extra money you do not want to save or spend, the HIPAA fines will take care of that for you…not trying to scare anyone, but there is a massive financial penalty for not protecting information, releasing information, and/or being a victim of a breach that contained privileged information on your client(s). Besides the financial costs, you have potential costs to your reputation.

Is the ROI current? Traditionally, an ROI is only effective for ONE CALENDAR YEAR and then must be renewed by your client and/or guardian. If that ROI expired after one year and you have released information using that expired ROI, you have opened yourself up to liabilities. Like discussed earlier about covering your ass, in social services, as much as we want to help our clients, we must take steps to protect ourselves and the agencies we represent. If you have followed what I have written up to this point, you are in good shape. If you are confused, that does not disqualify you from social work; rather, I urge you to meet with your company's Compliance Officer and get a full understanding of your legal responsibilities concerning securing your client's privileged information.

I have alluded to it earlier, but PHI can be ANTYHING. What is PHI? It technically stands for Personal Health Information, but really, it is anything that identifies the person/client as a recipient of a service associated with your organization. I can assure you, yearly, the idea of PHI will change. You as a social worker must be willing to keep up with changes in technology, restrictions, breaches, what is protected, what needs protected, because change is constant in social services, and it's not our clients' responsibility to adjust to this change. We are the professionals; therefore, we must be willing to adapt and comply. Seriously, we are responsible for our actions. I had a professor who said, "I will enforce the consequences of your choices—good choices equal good consequences and bad choices equal bad consequences," and that is so true in our profession.

Let's return to hurt feelings. A caller asks you and/or your agency for information. You can check in your system to verify that you have the client, but you do not tell them you are checking. If you have that client, you check to see if there is an ROI for the person/agency calling. An ROI must be specific to the purpose of the request; therefore, READ IT. If there is an ROI, see what can be disclosed and what you can answer. If you have NO *ROI* or what they are calling about is not in the scope, kindly respond, "I'm sorry, but I cannot confirm or deny that the person you are asking about is a client or not." They will get over it if they are professional. If you have an ROI and it is not specific to what they are asking, do you tell the agent that you have an ROI that is not specific to that? *No!* Your client is asking you to keep certain information. Perhaps doing so will cause them to call back and realign their conversation with the ROI. It is your job to protect your client; it is their job to ask what they want and get what you can give and nothing more.

I cannot stress this enough: an ROI that is produced that is NOT SIGNED and/or NOT DATED is NOT VALID under any circumstances! Sloppy paperwork is not acceptable in social work. We are stewards of our client's dignity, integrity, and likely safety. If you do not lose sleep over ROIs, you are not fit for social work or likely any health-care field! That last statement should not scare you away; rather, it should get you thinking about your own information, who has it, why they have it, if they should have it, and what rights you or your clients have to cancel the sharing of information.

Yes, your client can stop information from being shared. It is called revoking the ROI. Here's the tricky part. If there are multiple agencies with their own ROIs on file for the same purpose, all of them must be revoked for this to totally happen. For example, your client asks you to revoke the ROI for Specialty Practice in Anytown, USA, and Specialty Practice, due to their compliance standards, also requires your client to fill out an ROI. In order for it to be totally revoked, it must be revoked on their end as well. Follow this. Your client revokes with your agency. That other agency calls or contacts you, and they have a valid ROI. Can you share? NO! Why? Because your client revoked your right to share; therefore, you have to notify your client that you have received a request for an ROI from the said agency, that you know they revoked with you, and ask them to revoke with the other party. If you respect the other agency's ROI, you are in fact disrespecting your client, and you are in the wrong at that point. In fact, you may NOT even call that agency to tell them it was revoked. Again, the act of contacting would violate the PHI of the client.

Clients rarely understand ROIs. It is your responsibility as a social worker to inform your clients how best to fill out an ROI—do

NOT fill out for them. Let's back up. You can prescribe the purpose and indicate what needs initials and where to sign and date, but your client and/or guardian must be the ones to complete the ROI. If you are going to talk to a landlord, is there ever a need to talk about HIV, genetics, and/or mental health? Not likely. Is there a need to talk about alcohol or drugs? Only if your client has a known conviction. You know there will be a credit and/or criminal record report, and you want to advocate for your client about those issues. Also, just because an ROI lets you discuss does NOT mean you have to discuss! I have had clients who would not accept my advice on what to initial, and in those cases, I affirm their choice and explain the implications of such choices.

In my Case Management nerding, I was meeting with a US veteran who provides veteran Wrap Around services and told me the story of how when he was starting out as a Peer, other agents would ask him to discuss a client and would get mad because they would provide an ROI. The ROI as he reported allows him to discuss but does NOT mandate him to discuss. Our clients are granting us sacred information. We are the professionals, and they trust we are going to do what is best with that information. If what you are going to do will not help and/or advocate for your client, ask yourself, Should I do it? If you are ever curious, ASK your supervisor or make friends with your Compliance Officers, or at least know who they are and how to reach them.

As you can tell, much time has been devoted to ROIs in this discussion because there is a financial, legal, and ethical penalty associated with doing this wrong. Do not get me wrong, the legal and ethical reasons should matter, but the last time this social worker checked, paychecks are not meant to pay fines for unprofessional behavior! The thing you must understand is, your clients' information is privileged for all time. If you go to another place of employment, you cannot bring records with you. If you transfer to another division or transfer their care to another worker, you are done. Snooping in their chart if you do not have a specific purpose and/or reason is a violation.

I will never forget I had received very personal information in my mailbox on a close client all of a sudden. I had no reason to have it. This person was not engaged with my services. Finally, I tracked down who had sent it to me. I had expressed that I was not comfortable receiving this information because the need to know was not present. I returned the documentation and asked them to maintain or refer the most appropriate source. In reality, this information could have been passed to a Supervisor to create issues for the staff member. I knew I was not in a position to receive it; therefore, once I learned who sent it to me, I returned it to the original worker and ensured they understood not to return it to me.

Although not directly on the subject, secure your faxes, copies, and e-mails. If your agency gets faxes, have a person who is in charge of receiving them to get them to the right people. If you print something with your client's PHI, if you do not have a badge to sign in to retrieve that information, IMMEDIATELY go to the printer to receive it. If you leave it on there and others get it, you have betrayed your client's trust and are guilty of unprofessional behavior. If you send e-mails, DO NOT put your client's name and/or PHI in the subject line! Also, if you send an e-mail outside of your agency, SECURE IT because that protects you and your client. Where not directly related to ROIs, the impacts are the same. Did someone see something, get something, or do something that was knowingly and/or unknowingly in violation of your clients' trust in you as a professional (as I have written about above)?

I remember at one point I received an e-mail about a client. The e-mail was clearly sent to me in error, yet it contained all their PHI. First reaction, I called the sender to report the violation and asked them to send a retraction e-mail; the result was being asked to just delete. First, I did not open the e-mail because the subject indicated it was not intended for me, and second, I spoke with my supervisor to determine what was needed by my agency's standards to do anything about receiving unauthorized PHI. I will not declare what my supervisor mandated because your Compliance Officers may have a different standard, and the goal of this book is not to train you to believe my methods and/or supervisor are correct. At the same time, this e-mail error never had to happen, should not have happened, and could have been a costly HIPAA error in the wrong hands.

When I worked as a Social Service Director for a skilled nursing home, every fax and print was open-access for anyone who had keys to the copy room. Yes, the copy room had to be opened with a key, but that did not limit the information to need-to-know individuals. If you believe PHI is open-access and you do not need to protect your clients' information and identification, you are opening yourself to fines and penalties.

I want to detour again for a moment. If you are using laptops, tablets, and/or phones for your work involving clients, make sure it has encryption and security. You are the professional and are responsible for protecting your clients' data. If you have printed or received hard copies of PHI, lock it up. Notice, I did not say lock your office! Locking your office is not good enough. If it is in a bag/briefcase, lock the bag/briefcase. If it is in your office, lock it in a file cabinet AND lock your door. Security is about layers and ensuring you are doing the right thing with your clients' data. Furthermore, if you text your client, LIMIT what you write. Your phone may be protected; however, you do not know what protection they have on their end— you may have breached their trust with details others can access. I cannot say it enough: Cover your ass! Social work is about helping others, but at the end of the day, you cannot help yourself and/or family if you lose your job because you betrayed your clients' trust and compromised them.

I am not going to tell you I have never had a HIPAA violation. Rather, I am going tell you how I embarrassed myself and had to report my violation. Working as the Social Service Director, I had sent an "encrypted" message to the patient's insurance company and got a phone call—"I see that you attempted to encrypt the message, but I did not have to log in to access"—and sought help with this. I had done the right intention but failed to execute; I did not spell the specific word that would encrypt the message correctly, and the computer did not "catch my human error." Rather, a human who did not understand how I attempted to do right, which did not work out correctly, caught my error. I reported it to the Administrator as an unintentional HIPAA violation and made a corrective action agreement to prevent it from happening again in the future. What he did with my self-report is not known as it was not my duty to inquire. I tell this story because being embarrassed is not a reason to hide your violation(s). That insurance representative likely reported my HIPAA violation to their Compliance Office. Failure for me to self-report to my Administrator could have created any number of professional headaches.

Should you become a victim of phishing e-mails, NOTIFY your IT department IMMEDIATELY. The longer you wait, the more damage will be done. I might add, if you choose to open your personal e-mail on a workstation and that action corrupts your workstation, you own that risk. Understand, accidents happen. But as a professional, there are no accidents; rather, it is more like you failed to slow down and ask if the link was corrupted or if the message was from the sender. And in being busy, you compromised the well-being of your ethics and client. Being written up for a violation is far better than the financial penalties you could face! In fact, if I am honest, my spelling error as discussed above is not an accident any more so than being a victim of a phishing e-mail. I cannot tell you how important it is to slow down, ask questions, and be professional.

One way I avoid being a victim of phishing e-mails is not open-ing strange things on my work cell phone. If I do not recognize the e-mail, I will open it on my desktop/laptop where I have a great-sized screen and ability to fully see. I will even forward these e-mails to IT to ask them if it is real. In fact, IT came and did a training not long ago. I thanked them for not making me feel stupid for sending it, and then he said, "By the way, that was a test e-mail used to see who might fall for a phishing e-mail." They did not tell me when I asked for clarification about this e-mail if it was a test; rather, they told me not to open it and ensure if I forwarded to my manager not to for-ward the link so others would not by mistake click on it and infect their computers/systems. Just like social service agents need to cover their asses, your IT division will do so with test e-mails to help you become more aware if you are a "victim" of their tests.

I want to go off course a bit more. *REPLY ALL* is a hazard just as much as sending to the wrong LISTSERV and/or person. Social work is busy. We have large cases most of the time, and we want to accomplish a lot, but seriously, if you do not slow down, you create harm. Ask yourself, Is EVERYONE listed on the e-mail needing MY RESPONSE? Yes, they may all *NEEDED* the initial information, but is your additional responded information in excess of what some may need? This last statement is why using LISTSERVs is hazardous. Yes, there are times that information to a wide audience is necessary, but when the information contains PHI, you best know every person on the LISTSERV or do not send it that way; send it to each person instead. Remember, client information should be a need-to-know basis. This is especially true when talking about 42 CFR Part 2—protected information.

I remember a top member of the management had sent a message to a person. It was not received by *that* person but by the wrong person. It was received by his father who was a "senior" when it should have gone to the "junior." And the only reason it was not a problem, by luck only, was because NO *PHI* had been in that e-mail. Had that manager sent PHI, that person would have been required to notify Compliance of the breach. The fact that this manager shared this story created credibility with me as a junior associate. She never had to disclose her error; doing so was meant to prevent someone else from making a similar error and allowed me to write this to you. Let me stress. Managers, if you make a mistake, the mistake can be shared as a learning moment. Share it because it could prevent your junior associates from doing the same, just as sharing my spelling error that caused failed attempts to encrypt PHI in the e-mail.

If you are sending an e-mail, check if everything is correct about that e-mail address, that the specific person is correct, and if going out of your agency, SECURE it for sure (especially if it has PHI). This applies to text messages as well. Make sure you have the RIGHT NUMBER and *LIMIT PHI* in the text message. An ounce of prevention is worth everything. Social work is fun and exciting, but it is a profession, not a hobby! If my exposé on ROIs is your first reading, I pray that you have been challenged to dig further. I fundamentally believe books alone can be written on data security and client information. This is not an exhaustive chapter; rather, it is meant to get you thinking about it. If you have not thought about these things, as a professional, you need to. We will discuss later about education necessary to be a social worker, but understand, no amount of education can fix careless errors associated with ROIs, e-mails, texts, and data. None of these errors are excusable and justifiable, but rest assured, you are human, not perfect, but must be coachable of your mistakes! Own your mistakes, and when possible, report yourself first.

One more thing to cover: when talking on the phone, believe there are other ears! There could be ears in your office area or your surroundings, and your client might be in mixed company. How is what you are saying going to affect them if others hear? Your clients expect us to be professionals. They do not want everyone in the office to know about them, they do not want the people around them to know about them, and frankly, their well-being might be jeopardized by what is heard. Clients are not getting social services because they can figure things out on their own. Therefore, please be professional in everything you do. Seriously, if you must answer a call and are with a client, disclose, for example, "Matthew speaking, in mixed company" to signal to the person you are speaking with that there is a client and/or other ears present. It falls on the receiver to adjust what they tell you, and you are only responsible for what you say that others can hear. When it is all said and done, all these areas are relevant to ROIs and being a true professional.

I might add, common areas of the office are not meant to conduct official business. Managers, common areas are not where you do coaching and discipline any more than the common areas are used to discuss your clients. There should be soundproof offices and/ or meeting rooms. If you do not have this, arrange to rent a space to meet this need. Your clients are expecting you and your agency to be professional. If the common area is used, it needs to be an area that is secure away from other clients and/or parties who are not privileged to the information.

A client asked me to meet them at a local university campus. I explained that this space is very open and that their information can be heard by anyone who walks by. I gained their permission to meet and discuss their case. That person had agreed because they were comfortable in that setting, and as a professional, I had done my duty to ensure that their information was notified as open to the public. Sincerely, I would have preferred a more secure place, yet that client was comfortable and open—that intake was productive and meaningful. Let me challenge you. Do not let your idea of meaning and professionalism define your client's experiences.

My client Kim told me that at one point she had memorized my number and I was the only person she could call. She did not alert me she was in danger, but she knew I was a safe person to contact. Sadly, as Kim got established on her own, she said had her perpetrator known she was talking to a male, he would have beaten her. Assume every conversation with your client is a sacred moment; actively listen to see if you can pick up that they are in harm's way. I am not asking you to assume anything; I am asking you to engage at a higher level of understanding. If you know you are working with a client in a compromised situation and you are getting a call from them, maybe discuss with them face-to-face away from another person or ask them for a code they can provide you that things are not safe or need to remain sensitive. Just like a 911 dispatcher understands it is a real emergency when a pizza is being ordered, be prepared to empower your client to talk to you in a way that might save their lives or at least keep them from receiving a beating.

One more thing, if you are on a conference call, please identify yourself each time and wait to be recognized. Why? Information is processed by humans unique to each person. If you start speaking without being recognized or they do not know who is speaking, this leads to credibility issues. If you cannot tell, credibility is an important aspect to becoming a rock star social worker. Once you have lost your credibility, nothing positive can happen. If you leave your workplace of practice, the HR department may not be able to discuss your credibility flaws, but other cohorts and licensing/credentialing boards can and will. Credibility matters, and ROIs matter! If you are careless with ROIs, I cannot trust you will take anything else seriously.

I had a client who brought a specific issue to my attention because I was going to be attending a meeting where I could discuss this and asked if they could send a text message giving permission to discuss the case being that a formal ROI was not capable since we were not engaging before my meeting. Ideally, that text would not allow an organization to discuss with me; rather, it lets me discuss this client with an organization and demonstrate that permission to release their information and specific purpose to the organization (as I had requested specific purpose and organization to be listed in that text). Sometimes, you have to be creative and proactive as a social worker.

As this book had been concluded, this chapter had become real in my personal life. My Father was put into the care of a psychiatric residential care facility, and due to issues with his care, he had become hospitalized. Upon further research, it became clear his "care" was not being granted at the level the family and I had placed him there to receive. I notified the facility that as my Father's Legal Guardian, he would not be coming back to their facility. The comment made was, "We will call up to the hospital and check on him." This experienced social worker and family advocate realized he was no longer their resident; therefore, they had no need to call and get information for his care. En route to the hospital, I called and spoke with the Charge Nurse and gave a verbal revoking of any ROI/information concerning my Father and this facility. Had I not been quick to think, the facility would have been granted privileged information on my Father's care and the hospital would have been correct to give it even though, ethically, the facility should have realized they don't need to know something on a client who's no longer their resident.

Throughout this journey, I will ask you to nerd. If this is your first experience with ROIs as a professional, please take time to better understand this topic. Also, like a driving license allows you to drive until revoked and mandates you to maintain understanding of changing laws, you will need to be willing to continue to learn about ROIs and what changes may happen. Remember, the 42 CFR Part 2 is a higher standard of disclosure than traditional HIPAA. Before you disclose, ensure that you are not violating 42 CFR Part 2 while being in compliance with HIPAA.

This chapter has not been solely specific to ROIs; rather, it has been the start of the conversation concerning information, communication, and professionalism. As an advocate for my late Grandma and Father, I am afforded some privilege to release their information without their consent. I can have conversation with parties that influence their cases, provide insights, and not be required to sign ROIs because with my Dad, it is understood I am his Legal Guardian. But because of my understanding of this subject, I have been able to discuss when it may be beneficial for ROIs to be signed and when it is likely that Coordination of Care is the standard.

How to Communicate with a Deaf and/or Hard of Hearing

At this point, you should be noticing some themes—dignity and professionalism. This chapter is personal to me. I am hearing-impaired with a formal diagnosis of displaced eardrums and dysfunctional Eustachian Tubes. That is different than being deaf and more to come on this subject. But if you call a deaf person hearing-impaired, from all my experiences, they will be offended, and you will not be considered professional. Once you have lost professional status, it is hard to gain it back.

In social work, you may encounter technology without having to meet face-to-face to conduct your business with the hearing disabled or the use of sign language interpreter. When talking to a hearing-disabled person via telephone and they are using a service that signs back to them, first, ask the person doing the interpreting if they are following your speed and if they understand the language you are using and then speak TO YOUR CLIENT, not the interpreter. Also, we discussed ROIs previously. You do not need an ROI for an interpreter as they are an extension of the person and have their own code of ethics. It is important to understand, the interpreter cannot redisclose your protected conversation with your client (perhaps if something is not legal, that might change the dynamic).

If you are leaving a message, leave the message the same way you would if there was no interpreter. Because this writer values human interaction, I might say, "Interpreter, thank you for assisting." That is up to you. It is IMPORTANT that you speak fluid enough that the interpreter understands your words. If you are having a technical conversation, ensure that the interpreter understands the message/

idea because they are not signing word for word; rather, they are signing, in most cases, idea for idea. American Sign Language is its own language and does not directly translate word for word. That said, I have not needed for myself an interpreter to know if that is the case, idea for idea, but it has been communicated to me that way from the American Sign Language Interpreters assigned to assist my clients.

When having a conversation with your client and there is an interpreter physically present, TALK TO YOUR CLIENT and let the interpreter sign to them. Please DO NOT TALK to the INTERPRETER as it is your client you are both there to serve. It is your client who needs the information. Seriously, it is OFFENSIVE to believe that you can type everything out, write it on paper, or text the client everything instead of providing an interpreter. Beyond offensive, it is likely an ADA compliance issue. An organization can cut costs of doing business, but denying your client fair access to information that a non-hearing-disabled person has the right to is not equal opportunity. My Mom's stepmom was very hard of hearing. We would write everything out for Grandma, and we would verbally respond. That process met our immediate need for family to communicate with family. Please understand, how you do things in a family-like setting does not equate to a clinical setting. Family is far more forgiving than clients paying for a service—clients who are covered by ADA laws and expectations.

If you are in a situation where you must transport your client and an interpreter is not there because social work sometimes happens in the moment, ask your client if you can use technology, paper, texts, etc., but do not assume they will want this. When I was in high school, Mr. Manley put ASSUME on the board and diagramed it. It is ACTUALLY diagramed as this: ASS U ME, yes, it makes an ass out of you and me! Clients expect social workers to be professionals. Regardless if you are a volunteer, intern, or paid, being professional is not an option but a requirement.

Should you think these examples of communicating with the deaf are extreme, this writer has experienced them on the journey of social work. First time meeting with Alex, her children were not deaf like her. It is NOT OKAY to have children interpreting for the parent!

It might be necessary in an extreme but should never be a standard. I know we are talking about hearing disabilities, but children should NEVER have to interpret for parents who speak another language as well. If we are professionals, we will always conduct ourselves as professionals! There is one major exception. If that person's language is not a traditionally spoken language with access to interpreters, then you may need to have those who can translate (family) to do so.

The first encounter with Alex, the client's interpreter was delayed. I did get permission to write some things down for the client, but I explained it was for the moment only. Also, when a time to look at a house came up, there was no time to wait for an interpreter because housing market was tight and we had to act. Alex came with myself, and she agreed to let me talk to the landlord and text her back what was being said. Alex got to see the place and make a decision. In that moment, the lack of professionalism was actually warranted because the client had to move and needed to see available housing before another applicant would take from them. At the same time, it was also communicated to Alex why we did not wait for the interpreter, and the client understood and agreed. Failure to gain agreement from your client is not acceptable; we work for them and therefore must act professionally on their behalf.

Even though e-mail would be effective to communicate with a deaf and/or hearing-impaired person, it should not be your main way unless you do that with all clients. Marginalization goes against the standards of social work. Just because it is easier to write and some of us can type insanely fast, if we would not do that with a hearing-abled client, why would we treat a hearing-disabled client differently? This writer fundamentally believes in professionalism, dignity, removing barriers to client success, and when all possible, never marginalizing a client.

Let me be clear. Just because your client may not be able to hear what you are saying about them does not mean you can say it! How can we call ourselves professionals if we do this? Our clients, regardless of disability, trust us, and we must never compromise that trust. Also, if you are not willing to repeat what you said, DO NOT SAY IT to begin with—signed, myself! Seriously, as a hearing-impaired person, it makes me angry when people do not feel they need to repeat or they SHOUT at me thinking that will help. Both of those actions are not professional and will likely cause me as a hearing-impaired person to dismiss you. As a professional with disabilities, if I find offense in these things, how would a client who believes you are a professional react? Also, once you know I have a disability, you never have to reference it back to me. I do not reference to hearing-abled people that they can hear English (or their language of choice), so why would you start a conversation reminding me of what I already know? Instead, empower yourself as a social worker to meet that specific client's needs and provide first-class service. If I hear as a social worker that the budget does not allow for an interpreter (American Sign Language or other language), I will find the door and provide services somewhere that values the client.

Let me warn you, and we will discuss more specific to social work under scope of practice, if you are not trained and/or certified in sign language as an interpreter, do not offer interpreter services. Instead, identify that you know sign language and that you may be able to engage in a conversation. Language interpretation is a specific tool that requires specific training and competency to advertise as capable of doing. Check with your specific agency for their expectations of any interpreter-based offerings, but your clients should never have to go without this tool—cut costs somewhere else, but not on an equal access of services measure.

I expressed earlier that your client's children, both clients who are deaf and/or who speak another language, should not have to interpret for their parents but failed to explain why this is the case. In social work, we are discussing likely mature ideas. Children have enough trauma in their lives, and we social workers should never create additional trauma by asking children to relay adult conversations that are not necessary for them to be involved. As professionals, we must do better than this!

Finally, it is okay to ask a hearing-disabled person if they understand. No client should ever be in a state of confusion because they cannot process what another client without their disability can process. That said, what we do in social work can be complex, confusing, legal, and mindless—that is different than a client being confused because the information was not accessible to them. I fundamentally believe in fair and equal access and meeting my clients where they are. Just like the previous paragraph, children may not understand the concepts that are being asked to interpret in addition. Like noted above, it is not appropriate to expose them to the trauma of adult issues.

If you have never thought about your communication with an audience who cannot process what you are saying, I hope this gets you started in thinking about your message and audience. If your audience cannot follow the message, it does not matter how nice that message is or how well it was presented; it is a failure, and in social work, failure is only an option because the client quit, not because the client was not empowered. As a communication scholar, I learned that there is encoding and decoding of a message; what the sender is encoding is not always what the receiver will decode due to noise in the transaction. I am not asking social workers to be responsible for the noise affecting the decoded message; rather, own what you encode and ask your client(s) if they understood what you are trying to say.

Let me end this segment this way: every deaf person who has received social services from this writer has been willing to help make the exchange possible and the outcome beneficial. If you are humble, believe in the dignity of the person you are advocating; that will go a long way. If you identify that you have never worked with a deaf person and that you want to know how best to support that person, you will go far. Just like each client is unique, their issues are unique. A deaf person is unique, and the only thing consistent about them, from deaf person to deaf person, is a hearing issue. What you must understand is, a deaf person is still human, and they have the same emotions as a non-hearing-disabled person. If you are to be told that deaf people have the same emotions, please take a moment to ask yourself, Why is this news to me? And then continue reading this presentation.

Let me repeat: save money elsewhere, not by violating a deaf person and/or person who does not speak your language from receiving a proper interpreter. The damage to your reputation and the company's reputation will never be undone. Equal access to quality social services is not an option.

Scope of Practice

Let's be honest, social workers are ambitious and well-meaning in most cases, but that can also get us in lots of trouble. Just as organizations have a division of labor to run smoothly, there is an additional layer to becoming a social worker—your scope of practice. In most cases, this is based on your education, credentials, and not up for debate. To help you understand, when this writer started out learning formal/paid social services, I was an Office Assistant. It was the eve of a Holiday, and there was no management in the building (at the time of this circumstance). A client called that they had lost their power, which was a tragedy for them, and my first answer was to help.

In helping the client, I exceeded my scope of practice, but in this case, I did not do anything wrong and will explain that as we continue. I took down the client's information and told them that I needed verbal permission to call the power company to ask them to call the client to see if there was a technical failure that could be walked through via phone. When you consider our ROI discussion, it was clear that without consent, I could not release the client's information. The agency I worked for later coached me to say, under those circumstances, getting verbal permission was good but better would have been to give the client the number for them to call, taking the ROI issues out of the running. Where's the scope of practice? As an Office Assistant, I saw a problem and attempted to help, but my role should have been to transfer that client to any Case Manager available as they had the training to know how to advocate for the client and because I did not have access to the portion of the EHR to properly document the encounter. It was a missed chance to properly get credit as an agency (bill for it) and document what was accomplished for the client. Remember our discussions of documentation: if you fail to take credit for your work, seriously, nobody will give you credit for it; they will certainly know if you missed the mark in your documentation!

That encounter as an Office Assistant helped me become a better social worker once I was promoted to QMHA. I learned how to communicate with the office assistants, knew what they did and why they did it, and learned that even though I could do some office things, it was best for the Office Assistants to do it because they had specific access to areas of the EHR that a QMHA did not have and vice versa. If you understand, scope of practice is about everyone knowing what they do and doing what they do, and in doing so, the client wins. It then works out well. Furthermore, as a QMHA, I would exercise caution to make sure that things were done correctly. It is important that social workers are willing to take risks, yet these risks need to test your ability to do more than you thought you could, but not exceed what you are trained to do or what your license prohibits you from doing. A social worker or geriatric/health-care worker trying to do good can overstep and be accused of practicing medicine; you do not want that charge!

In my work as a QMHA, I had times when I would go to the QMHP (Qualified Mental Health Professional/therapist) and ask them to talk with the physician (Licensed Medical Provider/LMP) about a concern. Is there a rule that a QMHA cannot ask a physician a question? No, but the QMHP works directly with the physician, and the QMHA follows the direction of the QMHP. When you recognize the chain of command, it will also keep you in the scope of practice. Also, a QMHA suggesting something to a physician can create a question of intention. The question of intention can be talked through with the QMHP either in Supervision or staffing of concern and then professionally communicate the concern/idea to the physician. As alluded to moments ago, your intentions might be questioned by the physician as an attempt to practice or influence medicine.

As a QMHA, I was one of select credentialed staff who would help clients with their medication minders. This was a delegated task. We were trained by an RN and supervised by the immediate manager. Access to the medication room was restricted to us few, and we, who were cleared for it, could not grant others access in the medication room. We were trained that clients had to load their medication minders and had to know what and why they were taking their medications. It was not our job to put it in for them (if we did put the wrong meds, it is our mistake), but we would monitor that they did not make a mistake and help them call in their medications to the pharmacy. If a client was going to run out of meds, we had to call the RN and ask how to help the client not become medically compromised—we never told clients they would be fine, it's only XYZ medication, etc. as that is beyond our scope of practice. What social workers need to know about scope of practice is (1) it employs people, (2) it protects you from exceeding your training, and (3) it is in the interest of our clients. In fact, everything a social worker does, if you have not caught on, should be about your clients. Yes, you will gain something, but it is client-centered.

You may have an understanding of your clients' diagnosis (mental and/or physical health), but unless you have a medical degree, keep your mouth shut. No, that does not mean you should be void of compassion, but just because a medication works for you or a treatment did not does not mean it will for your client (or not be the right treatment). Rather, talk to the QMHP if possible, or staff directly with the LMP what your concern is (if in the same agency or if not and you have an ROI allowing it), and let the LMP treat your client. Just because the medication this writer takes for bipolar patients works does not mean it will for my clients; just because my bipolar nature shows one way does not mean everyone with bipolar will too. Again, we discussed earlier about each person being unique. Our diagnosis may be the same, but how it affects us is unique. If the social worker understands the expectations and the goals of their service, listens to their clients, and does not exceed their scope of practice, in most cases, the client will win, but in all cases, the organization is void of harm.

When I advocate for my Father, I explain to the doctors that I am also bipolar, and I suggest treatment that has helped me and let them know. They have the medical degree. I am trained not to practice medicine and believe the same applies to my Dad. We have honest communication about what I know and what I have experienced, and they explain why they have not, cannot, or maybe will not attempt that treatment. I am unique in my bipolar just as my Father is unique in his mental health failures.

Scope of practice is not meant to limit your understanding but rather to protect you from potentially being accused of practicing medicine or other unethical behavior. Social workers attempt to do well in their intentions as discussed in the first part of this chapter with my Office Assistant example. However, our clients bond with us, at times tell us things, and it is so easy to want to be a counselor to them when rather we need to remind them that they can talk to us but we cannot counsel them as we are not trained for this. If your client asks, "Do you think I have XYZ diagnosis?" it is in your interest to refer them to QUALIFIED medical providers who can answer that. Just like when clients ask us social workers for legal advice, DO NOT DO IT!

Let's discuss legal advice issues. Do you not understand how many levels to law practice there are and how quickly you can get into the weeds? If your client has an attorney, always refer them to that person. Having multiple people advocating for you is not a bad thing, but having the wrong advocacy can be harmful. If your client is not happy with their legal counsel or is not happy with their medical team(s), you can help them find new teams. That is in your scope of practice and ultimately is the right thing to do for your clients. There will be greater discussion to follow on what we call Wrap Around services.

I will never forget when Brandon had asked me, "Can I claim my children on my tax return?" They were in his home for a period that tax year. Seriously, you might know the answer, but unless you are the tax adviser, their legal counsel, or a specific qualified person, do not answer this question. I had let Brandon know that I am not trained to answer this question and that if I did know the answer, I would not provide it, and Brandon respected this answer. Seriously, your clients will ask questions that they have, and they will not always filter if you are the right person to answer. Rather, they will believe you are their support at that moment, that you can provide insight to their question.

It is very important to ask yourself, Am I the right person for this, and am I operating correctly? If you regulate yourself first, chances of others needing to regulate you is less. In most cases, you will receive formal *Supervision* in these roles. It is important to accept honest feedback that will help you become a better social worker. Frankly, seeking *Supervision* is better than getting *Supervision*. Many times, my Supervisors will get an e-mail asking if I can meet or if their door is open, see if they are available. I will discuss what is on my mind, what I need from them, and ask if they can provide feedback now or later.

Hardly can it be said enough, scope of practice defines your practice. You can always do below your scope but NEVER exceed. In school, we were challenged to do our best, do more, but in social work, this will never end well. The Army's motto "Be All You Can Be" should be your client's objective, but not the way you execute your job. As we have discussed about ROIs and PHI, it can result in financial and ethical penalties; the same is true for your scope. Not one supervisor ever called me out for asking about my scope, and a good supervisor will want you to ask what your scope is.

As a Navigator, my supervisor would ask me what my lane is. She did not do this because I was out of practice but rather because the expectations of the position were nonclinical, and she wanted me to master the objectives I was hired to accomplish. As a Navigator, I am not credentialed, as was when operating as a Certified QMHA, but the rules of scope of practice are still valid. Yes, I can provide QMHA-level Case Management and be in my scope of practice, but that is not my lane because my role is to point clients in the direction of resources, identify their barriers, and help them overcome those barriers. As promised, we will discuss Wrap Around services. The role of a Navigator is to help clients get services wrapped around them so when my services terminate, others are in place to help them. That said, social workers really need to help our clients become self-sufficient. I keep my Certified QMHA status year to year; however, I also understand that not every employment opportunity will use my QMHA and/or Case Management capacity.

While working as a Social Services Director for a skilled nursing home, I had more mental health training than some of the nurse managers I worked with. They would ask my opinion on how to meet the patient's needs. My advice was on a consulting level, never on a practitioner level. I understood my training and scope of practice and understood what I could tell them that would help them as nurses treat and communicate to the physicians for those patients' well-beings.

I recently got to sit in on a client's intake for Case Management concerning Wrap Around services after I leave the picture. The clinician said, "If at any point you no longer need me, I will not be offended, because my role is to help you reach the point where you no longer need my services." And that was awesome. This person was comfortable enough with their position (help the client better themselves) that they were not trying to create a nanny state for this client. This clinician did caution that if the client wants to terminate early, they might do a strength-based test with them to identify why it is too early but will respect their choice. In the chapter "Everyone Desires Dignity," I will discuss what it's like to be "fired" by your clients.

The moment a social worker believes they are the only human capable of helping their client, there are some issues. If you feel this way, please meet with your supervisor, discuss it in supervision, and know the client made it somehow before you and will need to make it after you. If you are in school, discuss this with your professors before it becomes a professional problem. It should be a point of honor to bring others to the table of client's success! Just because you do not like an agency and/or actor of an agency, that does not mean your client cannot gain benefit from it. Granted, if that actor and/or agency is not acting ethically, no question, stir them away. If it is your own personal conflict—get over yourself! As you can tell, as you go through the journey with me, there are times I am blunt and other times very compassionate. Life experience and diverse social work experiences have given me these perspectives.

It was alluded to earlier that a client may need help finding a new lawyer, doctor, provider, etc.; however, if you are doing this because of an issue YOU have with that person or agency, that is not an ethical behavior. There is a pharmacy in the area that had compromised my client's medication access multiple times. Since it was more than one client, I talked with other clinicians to validate my experience was not unique to my client interactions. It was suggested to clients why they should consider a different pharmacy. "Follow me," suggested, but not mandated. Our clients have autonomy, and if they choose to keep a failing pharmacy, that is their right, just as it's your reasonable duty to propose a better solution. If clients' behavior is not harming themselves but creates more work for you, deal with it. The autonomy of clients and maintaining scope of practice cannot be divided; once you violate either one of these as a social worker, your work becomes ineffective. If I have not offended you, great. If I have, please communicate why this offends you with your team. Sure, it is my experiences, but my experiences over the years with a variety of client encounters to justify it with multiple agencies.

As this is written, it is understood that my audiences may be diverse in years of experience or scopes of practice and want to learn what is social services. Social service is an idea, scope of practice is your mandate, and division of labor is what employs you. It is important that social service providers understand the idea, the mission and vision of where they are working, and their professional limitations. Once these things are understood, your clients will gain so much and your colleagues will gain. It is a win-win situation.

Let's discuss branding. It is worth putting in your e-mail and your voice mail your exact title because that will help people know what kind of social worker you are. Titles have meaning; your work will have meaning if others understand the scope. It is not the clients' responsibility to know your scope; rather, it is your job to maintain this and put the brakes on when necessary. Please do not say, "The client asked me to do this or wanted me to do this," because we will discuss later about power differentials. The client is trusting that you are doing what is right. We as social workers are responsible for our actions; clients are responsible for their actions. Therefore, we must never confuse this. Our clients will ask us to accomplish and do whatever we are willing to do on their behalf. Social workers are ambitious, good-hearted. It is our duty to control this to prevent unnecessary negative consequences.

We have discussed through this presentation the idea of professionalism. Whether you are a volunteer, intern, or paid social worker, you are a professional. Your ethos, your company's ethos, the body of professionals you claim to be part of are affected by what you do. Clients will, by human nature, try to get a social worker to solve all their problems or go further than they professionally can. By telling our clients we have limits, we are teaching them a valuable life skill. Fundamentally, social work is fun, but as fun as it can be, it is 100 percent professional. Just do not blame your client for your professional failures!

There are times that the social worker must be assertive and call out another professional, but understand, how you do this will either give you kudos or a bad reputation. As a Social Services Director for a skilled nursing home, I was also in charge of doing the discharge planning for patients leaving the nursing home (more in another chapter about calling clients patients). It was my responsibility before a patient left to ensure that home health was ordered and doctor's orders were sent to the discharging physician. Included in contacting the physician was to make sure all durable medical equipment were requested with all the codes and supporting documentation, received the orders back, and sent them to the right providers. Early on as a Navigator, a client of another staff member came into the office scared because their child was given a script for Albuterol and was told a pediatric nebulizer was necessary. The parent understood the script was sent to the pharmacy, and immediately I knew the problem.

First, pharmacies do not order or have nebulizers (in most cases), and second, the physician who treated their child failed to provide the necessary billing codes, O2 stats, and documentation required by the insurance company to pay for the pediatric nebulizer. As I had experience with this, in forty-five minutes, I had located a pediatric nebulizer in stock and learned they would process once the paperwork missing was faxed. I had contacted the physician and got what was needed and then had to drive an hour and a half to get it.

I remember my Supervisor asking, "Isn't there anything closer?" The problem is, yes, but that child was going to return to an acute setting without that treatment, costing insurance unnecessary money. It was a specialized product (pediatric nebulizer). Therefore, I told the supplier we were hitting the road, and by the time we arrived, insurance was approved, the product packaged, and the client given an orientation on how to use the machine. The physician should have known that this equipment does not get ordered without specific documentation, and the pharmacy should have communicated that the script was only for the medicine, not the machine. Nonetheless, due to knowing what the problem was and how to fix, that child was kept out of the hospital and the parent was happy, and this writer made an immediate impression on a new employer and coworkers, that what was said in my interview was fact—experienced and result-driven.

It would have been accurate to berate on social media the pharmacy and physician, but the negative impacts would have exceeded the gain. If you are in your scope of practice to fix what others have neglected do, please use that knowledge and understanding. Sincerely, always ensure that when you take ambition like this, you are qualified to do it because social workers are responsible for their actions.

This chapter has been very heavy on what not to do on purpose. If you understand dually division of labor and scope of practice limitations, you will go far, your clients will gain, and other Wrap Around providers will treat you like the professional you want to be. Your negative behavior is not isolated to yourself, your client, and/or your company. It can affect how other professionals will engage with you. As alluded to above, how you conduct yourself on social media will either enhance your reputation or make a negative mark.

The hardest part of being multidimensional as a professional is understanding when to apply that previous knowledge and when to curtail that understanding. No employer has ever asked me to ignore or forget what I previously knew. Instead, they have asked me to apply it specifically to that organization's purpose and needs. Just as when I advocated for my late Grandma and Father, I first identify my credibility and limitations and show the fact that I am willing to work with the team to meet my family's specific needs.

Boundaries Protect You

There will never be enough written about the need to be aware of boundaries in social work. Why? Most social workers are doing these jobs because we care about people and want to help. However, in doing this, we can easily lose focus on the Care Plan, Treatment Plan, goals, or objectives and start to become "friends" with our clients. If you knew a client outside of your agency before working with them as a social worker, disclose that to your leadership teams. Talk to your client about the restrictions that need to be put in place. If they have your personal cell phone from a previous encounter, kindly explain that they will need to refrain from using your personal cell phone and instead call the office and/or your company-issued cell phone. If you were previously friends on social media, you may have to delete them and/or suspend seeing their posts. At this point, you may be confused. How can we provide first-class service if we cannot be friends? You are missing something important. Being friendly does not require being a friend. Being compassionate, nonmarginalizing, an advocate, a caseworker, and/or a Navigator does not require friendship!

Let me share with you a professional experience seen but not directly applicable to myself. A social worker, outside of work hours, gives a client a ride in their car believing that the greater good has been done. First of all, using your own car, unless approved by management, puts you in a financial liability should there be an accident, and providing this service after hours has not taught your client how to be resourceful. If our clients never learn self-sufficiency, we have done a disservice. Eventually, you want your clients to close services and/or need you less than when started. There will be another client waiting for your services, so do not worry about running out of work.

I am about to be a bit more controversial, but it is well-meaning. If you do not accept this portion, that is fine and understandable. This writer is a fierce advocate for the LBGTQ movement, yet your clients should not need to know your sexual orientation and/or preferences. That said, if you are working with an LBGTQ person and you identify as an ally and/or member of that movement and feel disclosing your status will help them feel safe, then yes, that makes sense. Sexuality and expression of the social worker should be your business; your client's sexual behavior, unless it is criminal and/or negligent, should be their business. As a Speech and Debate Coach, I tell parents and the school it is not my job as the coach to know the sexual preferences and/or who my students are dating because there is no need to know this information. Seriously, speaking from the male sex perspective, when you start to have discussions about sexuality and you are not licensed as a counselor and/or therapist, you are starting to test boundaries and potentially put you out of scope of practice.

On a softer side, let's share a situation this writer found himself in. On lunch break, I was at the local grocery store. A client called, and I answered. She asked if I could pick up some primary foods for her. She did not know that when she called, I was at the store, so I told her, "Yes, I am already at the store. I can pick up, and you can pay me later." And that was an error that should never happen again. Why? I never got paid and never felt comfortable asking my client to pay me because I failed to establish when she would pay me and simply said. That was a boundary violation because I had used my own money to purchase something with the intent of being paid back. There was nothing illegal about it, but my power differential was so much greater than that of the client. This writer never recovered from that moment. Yes, I did continue to work with that client and made successes, but each time I work with that client, the question was in the back of my mind, *When would I get paid, and did I do something wrong?* We discussed earlier you will make mistakes as a social worker. The key is learning from those mistakes and accepting accountability for them as well.

I will never forget the day when I was transporting a client, "Marie," to appointments and had talked with her about how she might be splitting with her spouse and what plans we needed to make if this was the case. All of sudden, Marie called me a pet name. The nonverbal reaction I provided Marie must have been strong because she immediately apologized for it. That night, I had called every senior manager I could find to determine as follows: (1) Do I report this to the agency I am providing services? (2) Do I document this in the EHR? (3) Do I wait and discuss with my immediate supervisor in requested Supervision the next shift? I will not disclose how this went down because each company likely has a way to handle this, but it was communicated back to me that my reaction must have caused the client to know the pet name was not comfortable and demonstrated my intent to remain professional. Many times in this presentation, you will be reminded about being a professional because regardless if you are a volunteer, an intern, and/or a paid social worker status, failure to be professional is not an option. Just as it was not okay for Marie to call me a pet name, it is never okay for social workers to call their clients pet names. In geriatrics, we tend to call our residents nice names, and that is likely different, but even in those settings, you may want to check with your Administrator.

As one who is certified in CPR / First Aid, in addition to being Certified in Mental Health First Aid, if you have these certifications and you find someone who is in distress, you are legally obligated (not with Mental Health First Aid) to assist and remain until authorities with greater training come. To medically treat/triage someone and you expose their personal information, if done to preserve life, it is okay. To believe that you can do the same things when not in a life-and-death situation is morally, legally, and ethically wrong. Once you have lost your moral code as a social worker, it is even more difficult to regain your focus. On a similar note to losing your moral code, if you bill insurance and/or your clients for services not actually rendered, you need to forever remove yourself from social work as this kind of behavior damages our profession, company reputation, and yourself and causes harm to the client as well. There is no room in our industry for a second chance for Medicaid fraud—substantiated claims.

It is frowned upon to take pictures in our industry. However, I was working as a caregiver, and my contract was being paid by the State. The previous caregiver was reported by the client to have only sat on the couch and not cared for the home or person, and based on the condition of the home, the fact that the person had care seven days a week, it should have been spotless. I took pictures of specific details of the home, brought them to HR's attention, and deleted the pictures off my phone. The reality was, this caregiver should be charged with Medicaid fraud because they had reported they did the tasks and were paid for the tasks but failed to do them. I caution you, I was brought in to cover the shift and had not been in that home previously and not likely again; therefore, you never know when a good eye and demand for fairness will catch things like this!

Where I have done social work are small communities, large geographic counties but smaller cities. You will find your clients on off time. It is not okay to wave at them, greet them, or engage with them unless they have first engaged with you. At this point, let them introduce who you are and correct them if they say "This is my friend" in a loving way. Rather, say, "I'm a social worker helping her," but say nothing more. No need to say Navigator helping with her DHS case and/or Mental Health Case Manager because that violates your client's confidentiality. If I know where my clients work, in most cases, if there is another of that store or chain, I choose to go to the other store instead. Keeping your communication and engagement with clients professional as possible is best practice. Remember, just because you can talk with your client does not mean you have to talk about them.

Consider this. It is Christmastime or the cold season, and your client needs a warm jacket and/or their children are lacking gifts. What do you do? First, check with your supervisor and see if you are allowed to purchase something, and second, attempt to put them in touch with other providers. There is nothing that stops you from purchasing and giving to a provider in the community for them to give to your client. That removes the idea that YOU gave them a gift.

Careful, do not disclose your client's information without an ROI, but you can say something like this, "Please give to Matthew A. Eldridge's client who comes in and identifies that there is something on hold for them under Matthew's name."

As this is being written, marijuana is being legalized in more areas of the nation. If your client gives you food and you did not see it made, you may accept it, but DO NOT EAT IT because your failed drug test will not allow a defense that you got it from your client! Maybe explain to your clients before the holiday seasons that you would prefer not to have any gifts from them so it becomes a moot point ahead of time.

I love my friends and value my clients, but I never recommend my friends who are business owners to my clients. My clients may find them on their own, but if something goes wrong, your friend will attack you and client will attack you. Then you will lose a friend, and what remains is a client who believes you should have done more for them. When giving referrals, attempt to provide two to three referrals, unless it is specialty issue, then identify that it is a single referral on that basis. The reality most of us are in social work is because we want to make a difference. If you are in social work because you like having power, keep your friends, play power trips with them, and let another professional negotiate with the client's needs.

Housing is a huge need, yet my landlord owns my current home and property next to us. I would never tell a client if the property next door was available. If they found it and wanted to look at it, I would be obligated to show or navigate them to the property owner / my landlord, but it is acceptable to protect my address, my family, and not offer a client to live next to me. This sounds cold, yet being a neighbor to your client after they have received your services is very different than being a neighbor to your client before they have received your services.

I would hope it would go without saying, NEVER consume alcohol and/or any substances with your clients. In fact, if you have to take medications that are prescribed, do not take them, if possible, in front of a client. If you both take the same medication(s) and your client runs out, NEVER give them your mediations. It might seem like the right thing, but you are doing an illegal act that will not go well for you. Even if it is an OTC medication, if you give it to them and they have a reaction and/or die, you are the cause! We talked earlier about good intentions. Social workers must always have the best intentions because good intentions can cause boundary problems. In fact, if my students' parents allow them to take an OTC for headaches, I would never give it to them. They can take it and let me know they took it, but I would not accept the liabilities of having given a student this medication.

As a former smoker, I value the right of my clients to have a tobacco break. Yet I do not believe, even if I still smoke, that I would engage in a tobacco break with them. There is nothing stopping me from kicking it with them, but my clients do not need to know you consume tobacco. Besides, a client will likely ask you to share, and then you have to either say yes and create boundary issues or hard feelings because you would not give them what you have and are using in front of them. If you are a smoker, please do not smell like an ashtray before engaging with your clients.

If your clients do not already know, NEVER tell them and/or show them where you live. This seems like common sense, but sometimes, we as social workers can become comfortable in our dealings. Maybe you have an urgent need to use the restroom, and you would feel more comfortable going in your own home. Just do not do it. Your clients do not need to know where you live. On another note, if you are picking up multiple clients, ensure EACH client is comfortable with another client knowing where each of them lives. If one is not comfortable, arrange alternative transportation, and if you need to, explain they will have to pay for it. You are only doing what is requested of your client. Perhaps this sounds paranoid, but if I am transporting clients, I will not drive down the street I live on because someone might wave at me or call my name, and then it will be known that those people know me and/or established that I live there.

I know it might sound like a weird thing, but I really do not like to use my client's restrooms. Actually, their rooms and bathrooms are their personal spaces, and they make me uncomfortable.

In part, many clients' standards of cleaning are well below what I would accept, and the chances of seeing something that should not be seen are increased because they are not expecting a social worker in their personal space. Therefore, when possible, attempt to do your biological duties outside of their dwellings. I might add, if your biological need happens while your client is in your office, contact another office member to stay in your office to ensure your clients are not engaging in negative behavior or putting your reputation at risk.

Every organization will talk to social workers about this: your clients are not for your sexual gratification. Do not even think about it. The power deferential is so great that their ability to consent is negated. The reputation you ruin in yourself is profound. Their family members are not for your sexual gratification. Seriously, if you ever had a sexual encounter with that person before they were your client, you need to transfer them to another person because you are not capable of helping them.

I have spent less time on boundaries because your ethics trainer will provide increased discussions about boundary crossings and violations. I would encourage you to look at the definitions of boundary crossings and violations. Crossings will happen; however, violations are not necessary. A lot of boundary issues can be avoided by understanding your scope of practice, setting out the terms of the relationship with your client and frequent Supervision, and constantly looking for the Golden Thread in your work. More discussion of Golden Thread in the chapter "How to Interview for a Social Worker Position" and as we continue through this journey.

I want to discuss one final point on boundaries. You do not need to justify being off to clients (or even your coworkers). They do not need to know where you are going for vacation, what you are going to be doing, and how long. If you are having medical work done, you, too, have a right to confidentiality of your medical care. If you do this, you will secure boundaries with your clients so they know that your roles are the here and now, not every step and moment of your life. Think about this, if your clients know where you are going, they might try to find you there! It happens. Not only that, if they perceive you have money to do these things, they might be hostile against you for your privileges that they do not also get. Your personal life is that! Your self-care is just that!

We will discuss tobacco in later chapters (we started it in this chapter); however, if you are a smoker and your client is a smoker, ask your agency about the policy of having a smoke break with your client. Ensure that you are not violating break rules by engaging in too many smoke breaks with them, that you are allowed to consume tobacco with them, and be ready for them to bum a smoke from you and how you may handle that. If you do not want to share them with your clients, it's best to not even attempt smoking in front of them.

Later in this presentation, I will discuss how to empower your clients to find work, but I want to caution you to keep one thing to yourself: LinkedIn. I am a user of social media, but I never share with my clients that I am a LinkedIn user because I do not want them to stalk me on my professional social media (I recognize that writing this book may grant them means of finding me on LinkedIn). It is not private, and I do not restrict my settings. If they find me, that is on them. I do not have to add them, yet I use LinkedIn solely as a professional networking. What I post and appreciate on LinkedIn is night and day from my other social media platforms. It is okay to keep some things personal to yourself. One day, they may become professionals, but in the meantime, help them manage their current situation and remain focused on the Golden Thread.

In this chapter, I have dealt more with boundary violations. There are such things as boundary crossings where you will find mutual places of interest, maybe joining the same house of worship, shopping at the same grocery store, being in the same carnival, etc. It is natural to have boundary crossings with your clients. What is not natural or acceptable is engaging in unprofessional boundary violations. It would be impossible to tell you every boundary violation. The goal of this chapter is to gain self-awareness of how you are engaging with your clients. I cannot impress upon you enough, but clients who did not have a previous encounter outside of your professional role are not your friends.

I have discussed being professional much in this presentation, and it will continue. Being professional is also recognizing specific boundaries. Yet it is likely you are a social worker or entering this field because you want to help people. It is likely that you will encounter clients who have no family, or maybe if they do, their family cannot do what you may be capable of doing—being a match for medical reasons. No, I am not saying donate your sperm or your eggs to help make a baby (in fact, I would not endorse this); rather, maybe your client needs bone marrow, a kidney, or some other kind of medical transplant. Maybe there are no matches, then you decide to check your status, and you become a match. Check with your agency to see if you would be in the right of helping this. Do not do anything like this without your agency's approval; if you get approval and you want to help, ensure that you explain it is out of compassion that you are medically helping, not desire for return. Let me be honest. I am willing to do this for family, but I am not sure I could do this for a paid client because it would be hard to separate my professional relationship. That said, if a member of my church needed it, I would line up to help without even needing to discuss with my management team.

My Father has stage 3 kidney failure. If donating a kidney would change his life for the better and should I also be a match, it would make sense to act on his behalf. What social workers must understand is, when you are paid, an intern, and/or a volunteer, the methods of engagement must be totally professional and not simply acts out of our feelings. When I die, I am expecting my family to donate my remains to science and viable organs to those in need. I am not certain I want to release my identity and/or my family's identity as my act of donating organs, skin, and body to science is to serve a higher purpose, not to create unnecessary dealings with the family.

Dress to Impress /
Dress for Success

How You Dress Says Something

I have many examples of this that I want to share. As a Marketing and Admissions Director for an Assisted Living, I had worn a tie and suit jacket daily in my work. I was under the impression that as a manager, I had to dress to impress, and my coworkers attempted to get me to understand that I could lose the jacket sometimes and would still be professional. I struggled because my personal ethos "mandated" to look professional. As I fast-forward to modern day, wearing a polo shirt and slacks are just as professional. If you are the CEO and/or Executive Manager of a social worker program, yes, you may dress to impress, but when you are working with clients, you do not want to dress in ways that you stand out. Ladies, wearing pearls may seem eloquent for going to high tea, but your clients may not be comfortable with that because they are maybe wearing costume jewelry. Men, wearing shined, mirror-glazed shoes may give the impression that you are too good to get your shoes dirty. Frankly, I wear sandals and socks and connect with my clients and get results. Do I miss wearing a tie and jacket? Yes, to a degree, but when your clients feel comfortable with you, they will trust you, and trust is vital in our work.

I remember my Supervisor discussing dress code with me in *Supervision*. There was no reason to discuss other than he was telling this story. A person in the community called and said he saw one of the agency cars at the mall. He asked the person calling if he would describe the two people and if he could identify the employee of the agency and the client engaging with the employee. The caller could not, and that warned the boss; that worker was not doing anything wrong as they were doing legitimate skills training with the client and did not present themselves in a higher status than the client they were supporting. If you feel that you have to dress in fancy clothes, additional jewelry, etc., think about the message this is sending to your clients.

If it is jeans Friday at work, wear them because that will give you a chance to relate to the clients more and not stand out in the workplace. Clothing is a power statement. If you do not believe so, think about this. Joseph in the Bible was targeted by his brother not because he wore a coat but because his Father made him a coat of many colors, and that was more of a statement than what his brother got. I may take some heat for this. If you want to be an effective social worker, comb your hair naturally as possible, do not dye your hair with crazy colors, and watch your tattoos and piercings. Let me pause. If your ethnicity affects how you style your hair or how it grows, that is much different than purposefully making it crazy. None of those things will disqualify your understanding and knowledge, but they can compromise your ethos. I have spent much time in this presentation about your ethos and protecting it. Seriously, once it is compromised, it is nearly impossible to regain.

My own preference is the absence of tattoos, yet I have met some highly talented social workers with tattoos, and if I used my own paradigm to judge what they know or could teach me, my own success and future client successes would be harmed. I do not have piercings, yet if piercings do not detract from the ability to perform the job, so be it. Ladies, if you are wearing a ring and it has prongs and/or can cause people to be scratched, it may be best to remove it while doing geriatrics/social work and wear it on your own time.

Dress for the occasion: if you as a social worker are going to be doing a lot of cleaning and helping clients get organized, do not wear white and light-colored slacks, skirts, etc. Talk to your manager and see if you can have a revised dress code that fits the moment. I want to speak to some in the medical field quick. If you are providing care services and your employer does not require scrubs, do not wear them! Scrubs send a message that is hard to overlook when you are receiving care just like those shined shoes that are too good for getting dirty send. Furthermore, disposable gloves, such as latex exam gloves, can also send the wrong message to your clients. Certainly, if working directly with clients, you need to protect yourself, but if you are wearing them because you may be exposed to germs, and you are in social services, you will likely offend your clients. There is a difference between universal precautions and a desire to make people feel like they may have "something."

Let's talk holidays. When I was a dietary chef, I had to work on Easter Sunday. I chose to wear a chef's coat, and I went to the dollar store and bought a loofah and pinned it on my chef's coat to show the Easter Bunny had come to work with his tail. I will never forget one of the residents asked, "Can I pull your tail?" At that moment, because I dressed for the moment/holiday, I made some older person's day. What about other holidays such as Halloween? Dress up. Do not wear offensive clothing, but be part of it. When your clients know you are willing to have fun, that will change things for them as well. A client who is having fun trusts you. I promise, they will engage more. If you think that painting your skin another color during Halloween is okay because it is a costume, you are mistaken and are likely going to be considered offensive.

Stained clothing should never be worn in social work. Seriously, your clients are likely going to be wearing some of those same things, and they do not want to be reminded of the clothes they have if they actually made an attempt to wear something nice for that encounter. Take pride in how you look, but understand, clothing and accessories create power statements. Do what you can do to prevent these power statements. I am not asking you to look better than your clients; I am just asking you to take inventory and realize that if you look deprived like your clients may also look, the wrong message is likely to be sent.

Not long ago, I went to a State agency with a client. The social worker at the state was wearing a beer company beanie hat and helping the client. The social worker understood what he was doing, but the image was not professional. How can you work for the State and wear a beer company beanie and expect to be taken seriously? Why was that even allowed by management? If nothing else, take pride in what you wear and how you represent yourself. If you wear a T-shirt, make sure it is not offensive or not advertising something. You are not a billboard but rather a professional.

I hope if you have read each page, you understand that these are reflections from my journeys as a social worker, a geriatric provider, and an advocate for my family. I have not experienced everything but have worked in enough fields and agencies to have experienced enough diverse people and problems and successes to share them with you. I don't want to shame you for looking nice. As I noted in this chapter, I thought wearing a tie and jacket was necessary. I have come to a conclusion that wearing a tie and jacket is necessary when I attend Court for a client or maybe a meeting with a community partner on mutual engagement, but it is not necessary for interaction with my clients. If you are a Pastor/Clergy, you can determine if a suit and tie is what your audience values. As an undergraduate, I was taught about audience analysis; as a Graduate student, I was taught to create platforms for those audiences—social workers kind of blend in both of these academic ideas. We will discuss education in greater details later.

Dressing professionally is only half the job when you are a social worker. We must smell nice too. Caution: this does NOT mean taking a bath in your powder, lotions, creams, perfumes/aftershaves, etc.; rather, it means wearing some non-offensive deodorant in the spring/summer and taking regular baths/showers. Our clients will likely smell, more to write about that later; they do not need their social worker to smell. Again, cosmetic smells may trigger our clients' asthma, so be careful with this as well. On another note, if you are a tobacco user, *please* (I am a former user speaking about this) do not smoke right before getting your client. It is not a crime to smoke tobacco, but it is not decent to smell like an ashtray either (as I reminded you earlier).

Wear your badge! If you have a client that does not feel comfortable with you displaying your badge, put it in your pocket, but always keep it on you. That is your credentials. Explain to your clients it is part of your required uniform. Most clients are used to badges being worn, but those that have issues can likely be reasoned with. We have talked about ethos, and that badge is a physical sign of your ethos. Let me caution you. Do not leave your badge in your vehicle, where it can be easily seen/stolen, because some badges are keys to the building, and by the time you notice it is stolen, the damage might be done. When I come home, I take my badge off and put it on the key holder, and when I prepare to leave, I put it on before leaving the house.

On another note about badges, NEVER give your badge to your client or any other member of staff, including management, until you have resigned or ended your shift (if you are required to return them on breaks, lunches, and end of shift). That badge is yours, and you are responsible for that badge. It is a ticket to privileged information in many cases as most badges are also electronic access points of entry. If you lose your badge, file a report IMMEDIATELY just like you would if you lost your debit/charge card. All these things establish you as a professional. We will discuss later about education, but your schooling does not make you a professional; your character is what makes you a professional. Wear a fun yet professional lanyard if you choose. Seriously, your lanyard choice will say something about you. Is it a positive statement?

I want to caution you. When you go shopping on your lunch or after work, try to remember to remove your badge. I cannot tell you how many times that another customer believed I was an associate of that store because I was wearing my lanyard with my badge. Also, by wearing your badge, it gives you a chance to lose it. I was shopping one day, had lost my badge, and did not know it. The associate saw it had my picture, confirmed my name, and returned it to me. Because it was immediate that my badge was lost and returned, there was no need to report it was missing; had I learned after leaving the store it was missing, yes, a report would have been warranted.

I want to come back to the original theme of this presentation: "No Bad Days… I Can Eat This Pizza." By saying if your clients do not feel a power differential in your clothing choices, they will be comfortable eating with you, opening up to you, and will build trust in you. I dare say, tie and jacket would not have created results with my clients who broke through and found success. It is an honor to have a client feel comfortable enough to eat with you. Eating, like clothing, is a very personal thing, and if you are making people comfortable enough to get nutrition, I believe you are likely doing something right. My client would never have told me his worst days sober is better than his best days high if he did not trust I was genuine and caring. Your clothing choices will establish you as genuine or out of touch!

On another note, try not to wear pins and stickers that support a cause, a political and/or religious belief around your clients. What you do with your own time is that; your clients are not likely going to believe what you believe or think like you think. If you have something that triggers them, I am sorry, but you own the responsibility for the trigger; they own the responsibility for the reaction. If your agency lets bumper stickers be put on cars, keep them professional. I might add, if your personal car has political statements on it, it might be best to park outside of the parking lot where clients can see it. Ultimately, you will do what you feel is best, but understand, your actions have consequences!

I want to deviate really quick. How you decorate your office will say something about you. Are there pictures of family? Do you have spiritual statements and/or religious biases displayed? If you think displaying pictures of your family or religious biases in your office where clients can visit and get treatment/help is okay, you are wrong. If your clients know what your family looks like, you are making your family a target. Your clients will attempt to stalk you (I know this), and the last thing you need them to do is stalk your family! It is okay to be religious (if you are). Just do not make your office preach to your clients. Also, it is okay to be diverse in your sexual preferences, but your clients do not need you to wave it in their faces in your office either. Your office is not your house; it is a workplace with a purpose, and it is best to remember that.

I may offend you or someone else, but what you drive says something. If you are in a position where you use your own car, ask yourself what statement it might make. I grew up with a Senior Pastor whose income was tithe-based. Many of those attending that church, including my family/parents, were working-class poor. He and his wife chose to drive a Lincoln Continental, not a used one but brand-new or at least not very used, and they had a boat in the front yard, a nice truck to haul the boat, and a fancy house inside and out. I am not against having nice things; if you are getting nice things because of church donations, you should act and live as such. That same principle applies if you are driving to your clients' houses or engagements and use your own transportation. If that transportation is fancy and upgraded, think about what message that might say about you.

There was a manager from the corporate office who came to visit one day. He drove their vehicle that was expensive and out of touch with anything those in our office would be capable of driving. The corporate office had company cars that could have been used for business; had that person used a company car, we would not have marginalized this manager like he did showing up out of touch with the working members of the business. It is likely this person and their spouse had combined income to justify, yet we did not meet this person's spouse; we met this person on company business, and it created animosity. That said, this manager will likely never hear that animosity because we staff members would be embarrassed to express it, but we sure did express among ourselves.

Just because you like your upgraded transportation, it is best when engaging with clients to fit in. Just like the story earlier about my Supervisor asking the caller who reported the worker at the mall which person was the client and which was the worker, your transportation should not create power differential statements. If you are an executive working for a social service agency, I would say you are out of line to travel first class and/or to travel in a private jet for company business. Those *fake* religious evangelists who argue that they need special accommodations for flying are perverting the gospel message (so says myself) and are not recognizing how they gained the money to travel. If this segment has offended you, I ask you to analyze why you are offended. If you are a private business executive and want a private fleet, that is very different than an executive of a nonprofit and/or social service agency.

That said, if you are traveling on your own time, using vacation, or not doing company business, feel free to rent a fast, sexy, appealing vehicle. In fact, fly first class, maybe even take the train with special accommodations. Just be careful not to flaunt it where your subordinates have to know. In fact, it may not be recommended for anyone in management to join their subordinates on Facebook. How you spend your self-care time is your business; it is the company's business how you travel and accommodate yourself on its dime or your church members' dime.

When my Father was transferred to a psychiatric hospital, I had packed him some comfortable clothes that would also help him be human. Some of those clothes were branded athletic team apparel, others were comfortable pj's, and all of them were lacking strings and means of being used to self-harm. You can never overthink your actions and what message they send, especially when those actions are on company time and/or dime.

Do I Need a Degree to Be a Social Worker?

There is absolutely nothing wrong with getting an education! An education builds a solid foundation, expands your thinking, and introduces you to theory, practice, and application. Yet to be a social worker, a degree is not necessary, but to be licensed and/or credentialed in a specialty of social work, you will need degree(s) and/or certificate(s). If you are starting to think about school or are in the middle of getting your education, do it! Let me caution you against going into debt for a degree. Social workers who are not licensed as counselors and/or other types of QMHPs will not make the greatest amount of money, but for some of us, helping another human is enough. If you are a volunteer and/or intern social worker, blessings to you. At the same time, before you can become a QMHP, you have to first get your undergraduate and to be accepted as someone who should get their QMHP; you have to have some experience. It is true that you can go from your undergraduate directly to Master's, but those who have done so are not gaining the necessary experience to truly make the difference they could be making professionally and for our clients. Yes, Graduate programs will require an internship. I want to encourage you to become a junior associate before desiring to become a Master's level associate. Also, remember, I have a Master's right now in Business Administration, but not all Master's are equal. My business degree will not qualify me for a Master's level in clinical work, yet my business degree helps me express business-relevant information to clients and enhances how I engage with my employer.

To be a Peer Mentor for Drug and Alcohol, you have to attend a specific training that can certify you, and then you must comply with your credentials to maintain that certification. To be a CADC (Certified Drug and Alcohol Counselor), you have to get formal education, but not specifically a degree. To advance as a CADC, there are education requirements. To be a Case Manager, one will not always need a degree, but you must have sufficient work experience to justify your position. In other words, determine what kind of social services you may want to enter and learn what the credentialing is for these positions and/or what kind of education you may need.

As a credentialed QMHA, I never took a single academic course that led to my credentials. It was life experience (the school of hard knocks) and compassion, coupled with paid work involving those who have a severe and persistent mental health disorders. It is counterproductive and a waste of formal education to attend four or more years of undergraduate and have gained no intern or practicum experience and expect to become a social worker. The experiences you gain working with the people you want to help cannot be taught in this presentation, in any textbook, or in an academic classroom. Rather, real education is learned in the field. Let me be clear. If you are not a compassionate person but judgmental (unable to recognize your bias) and are on a power trip, social work should never be your calling. If you are coachable, want to help those who are underprivileged, and want to make a difference, you are already in the right mind to do this kind of job. If you have been where your clients and/or future clients are and are no longer there, do not get high and mighty about it; use your experiences to better your clients.

When I became a dietary chef, I did not go to culinary school; rather, I was trained in the kitchen of my undergraduate institution and learned how to blend flavors, seasonings, and products into something people want to eat and made magical things in the kitchen. Before I was a Resident Manager for a foster home, I had started out as a part-time Activities Director for that set of homes and learned how to do the paperwork, the OARs of foster care, etc. Those experiences helped prepare me to become a Resident Manager. In order to become a Resident Manager, I had to take the course and pass the test, but my college education did not make me a Resident Manager. What my college education did was teach me how to organize the paperwork into systems that made sense and were function-able. Without my formal college education, I would not have run the office aspects of being a Resident Manager well. I want you to understand, an education is prudent, a good choice, yet failure to be actively involved in the field and only relying on your degree will not properly prepare you for being a rock star social worker.

My journey as a formal social worker was in many respects by accident. I was a freight broker. Not liking what I was doing, I applied for an Assistant Manager position for a hotel. I did not get the job; however, the recruiter promised me she would help me find something. Shortly after, I was placed as a temporary employee in a community mental health provider as an Office Assistant, and then nine months later, I was promoted to QMHA. Your journey to becoming a social worker is likely going to be absurd, but when you consider your clients' stories, it may not be much different in real-ity. Had I not been willing to accept the risk of being a temporary employee, none of this writing would have happened, none of these experiences would be made. Social workers must be willing to take legal and ethical risks.

As I have developed these chapters, I reflected on my journey and realized I was a social worker long before I had the title. While an undergraduate, I had cooked a community meal once a week for the homeless and/or those experiencing food insecurities. We did not question their right to a meal; instead, we validated their human-ity. Before I did my practicum for the community organization, I had volunteered countless hours there as an Organizer to help other people in poverty rise above together. We had done food drives and toy drives for Christmas, and at one point, they challenged me to attempt to help Spanish speakers learn conversational English. My education did not put me in touch with that organization but rather my compassion and desire to help another person rise above poverty. My education allowed me to gain academic credit working for the organization with a prescribed mission and vision specific to that practicum experience.

I reflect on my years of teaching Sunday School and being a Speech and Debate Coach. Neither one of these titles are "social worker" titles, but the impact is equal to, if not greater than, a social worker. I am not asking you to agree with me, but seeing another person saved by grace and changing their life through the power of the Holy Spirit is amazing. As a social worker, I can validate a person's religious choices, but I cannot specifically engage with it like I can as Sunday school teacher. Likewise, as a Speech and Debate Coach, I have to be open and accessible to my student who is questioning their sexuality, gender, or even their self-worth. In other words, do not limit your understanding of social work by a specific title; let compassion and professionalism guide you on your journey.

What can you do to prepare yourself to be a social worker? Shadow! This goes back to the discussion of ROIs. You have to get permission from the clients to shadow with a social worker, but until you live the experience, you will never understand it. Just like the Case Manager who met with my client and admitted that she is okay being fired, she had an intern from the local college that day, and the intern had to gain permission to meet with my client and her new Case Manager. If you go from one organization to another, ask to shadow for a week to learn the culture of the workplace, how things are done, how to document your encounters, and be coachable. In high school, Coach Michael DeRobertis, who has since passed, took me aside on the track (to this day, I know exactly where I was) and said, "If you are going to be coached, you must be coachable." That encounter changed my life! Failure to be adaptable to your organization will not allow you to succeed.

You must understand the EHR that your company is using. If you are in a paid capacity, the EHR is how they document what is being paid; it is how you take credit for what you have done and learn what your limitations/settings are and who to contact for assistance. My first experience with an EHR was being an Office Assistant. I had done everything by hand previously; an exception was as a Marketing and Admissions Director, I put my leads into a database. You will likely *never* master your EHR, but for the portions you use daily, learn them, understand them, and ask questions about them, and you will learn that the EHR is your friend. In all my agency work, none of them have used the same EHR; the fundamentals are the same, but be open to learning how to navigate the functions you will be required to use. If trainings are offered on your EHR, enroll in them (with supervisor permission).

I will caution you not to do more than one social worker job at a time. Why? Conflicts of interest. Some of those clients, as we discussed Wrap Around services, might be getting services at the other locations, and then you have to prepare your mind to focus on what you know from that place versus what you know from the other place. Disclose any social work experiences you are doing to your employer (especially if being paid), and if you are volunteering, NEVER work as a volunteer for a client that is also receiving paid services from you in another capacity unless the goals and objectives are completely different! Most of all, I want readers to understand that having a degree does NOT qualify you for social work. It prepares you, but your qualifications are what you know, and we will discuss this in the chapter "How to Interview for a Social Worker Position."

A social worker must be able to read and write effectively. That said, you do not have to know how to spell well. Spelling is my downfall, but I am capable of seeing the errors and correcting them. Grammar matters as well. Those notes you put into the EHR can be subpoenaed, and if you cannot spell correctly, write correctly, or communicate effectively, your ethos is compromised! Make no mistake, this presentation is written for an English-speaking and English-writing audience. If you are of a different culture and language, work with your supervisors to determine how best to communicate in ways that do not compromise yourself and your ethos. If you are dyslectic, tell your supervisor; employers are willing, in most cases, to make reasonable accommodations. When I worked in retail, I was granted a name badge that identified that I was Hearing-Impaired, and that was my request so customers would understand that if I was not hearing them or asking them to repeat, there is a reason and not me attempting to be rude.

I want to discuss an important reason for going to school. An education will challenge you to get rid of a black/white thinking and let you understand that there are a rainbow of colors and shades of gray in this world. I cannot think of many times in social work that things have been black/white. Yes, there have been legal and ethical issues, but that is not what we mean by black/white versus shades of gray in social work. Again, you are the professional, and you will be asked to make decisions that are sound and reasonable. How you document those decisions will determine much. How you document those decisions will be influenced by the education paths you have taken or not taken. There is no one degree that prepares a person for social work; it is your heart that prepares you.

When my Father was alive, as my Father's Legal Guardian, I am asked to act out of goodwill and his best interest. I want to affirm that you will sometimes make decisions that will question the key, Did you act judiciously? Was it ethical? Are the intentions moral? Not all decisions will be life-and-death; some decisions are acts of service and determining who best can provide that service so you do not create an unnecessary boundary violation. While my Grandma was alive, acting as her Power of Attorney and advocate, the same principles had applied.

Let me discuss an elephant in the living room: an online degree for social work is just as effective as a face-to-face degree on campus. It is your internships and practicum that will have the great influences on that education to benefit you for social services. Let me leave you again with this thought: *no one degree* is best for social services; it is your heart. I cannot say that enough. If you do not have compassion and empathy but believe you are better than others or people deserve their situation and are negative and vindictive, please do all of us social workers and our clients a favor and do not apply or ask to join our profession. That said, it is okay to personally believe some people have brought their situations upon them. Self-sabotage happens; this writer has seen it, reported it, and told clients that was their problem. But clients need a champion who will defend their humanity, and if you are that person, come join me in my journey so you can one day have your own reflections.

I want to caution something I have seen: do not get a Master's Degree and believe that you can enter into Master-Level social work if you have not done basic- to intermediate-level social work. You have wasted your education and will not be as successful with your clients.

Clients do not care about your education. In fact, I have worked with clients with equal or greater degrees of education than myself, but the school of hard knocks hit them harder; they needed someone with clarity of the moment to help them. I am so pleased that my degrees were not clinical at the time of writing this and that my experience was genuine because that has prepared me for amazing things. If you have a good heart, as has been established is necessary, what you will also need is compassion. Our clients' ACEs and trauma brain requires compassion and understanding. Maybe you have never had an addiction issue yourself, never been homeless, never needed a food box, or maybe you have a sound mental health. You are blessed, but what will bless others is if you can try to listen without judgment and guide those clients to a point of success. It was established earlier that each human is unique and that your credentials and education and experiences are unique. Use that uniqueness to make a difference in your clients. Last thing to say about this is, if you do not believe in yourself, you cannot ask your clients or a prospective employer to believe in you!

It is not foreign to me that those in an academic institution reading this are likely in human services, sociology, psychology, or other types of social science classes. Maybe those reading are managers who have had their degrees for years, did social services, and are now promoted. The goal of this chapter, this book is to be a training tool to make the reader a rock star, seasoned social worker or help a manager empower their new associate to become that future rock star, seasoned social worker.

"My Client Smells"

Let me first honestly write, please do not laugh at this chapter's title because you have not done real social work until you have dealt with smells. I am talking about body odor, urine, feces, vomit, alcohol, tobacco, cannabis, manual labor, and there could be so many more. Let me take personal inventory because part of being a social worker is knowing our bias: (1) I have a house and/or safe/secure shelter, (2) I could have taken a shower today with hygiene products (if I had chosen), (3) I have clean clothes, (4) I have access to either a laundromat or my own washer/dryer, and (5) I have a sink to brush my teeth using my own personal tooth brush. Seriously, I think you get the point. If these five observations are true for you like they are for me, you likely have more than a majority of the clients you will serve in social work. Social work is not pretty; we deal with the ugly side of life. Have you heard the saying "Putting lipstick on a pig"? Well, welcome to social work.

I had told an associate at work I had written this chapter, and they laughed because they knew exactly what I was talking about. If you are laughing because you want to marginalize the client who smells instead of laughing because you know these experiences, I want you to check that behavior before proceeding with this chapter.

Just like discussed in hearing disabilities, others and myself who have a hearing disability do not need you reminding us that we have a disability any more than a client who is not well-kept needs a social worker reminding them that they are unkept unless you have a solution. Solutions? Well, we will talk about solutions under the chapter titled "How to Interview for a Social Worker Position." This chapter is about the humanity of the person we are treating and/or providing a service. Frankly, it is okay to document that your client is not well-kept or they smell and what that smell might be related to as that documentation may be necessary to substantiate that they are no longer capable of caring for themselves. Understand that your observations and documentation are not points of judgment; instead, they might be a means to getting your client help should guide how and why you document the specific observations seen and learned. Our documentation as social workers and geriatrics specialists should always be fact-based, void of opinion, and not based on our qualifications to cast such judgments.

When a client who smells gets in my car, I will never roll down my window! Instead, I roll down the back windows to allow fresh air to come into the car. Only after the client rolls down their window will I roll down mine. I am certain that the client can smell themselves; it is likely they are so used to it. But still, I am confident at some point, self-awareness happens. By rolling down mine and/ or their window, it is bringing attention to the fact that they smell. Social workers are not in the business of marginalizing our clients; if you are, then you need to find another profession (I cannot express this enough).

If I am bringing a client to my office, especially if I have a window, I might send a text and/or e-mail to the Office Manager asking them to open my window or door only if office is lacking a window that could be opened BEFORE I arrive. I will not tell them who is coming with me because that is a need-to-know basis, if you remember that discussion from earlier. Just as I will not open my car window on a client, I do not want them to see me opening my office window. You might be asking about security. Remember, your desk and office should NEVER have PHI lying around to begin with; it should be locked up, and your computer should be secured. Therefore, the Office Manager going into your office or anyone else during this period would not create a HIPAA hazard. Just when you thought clients' PHI and securing their records were isolated to its own chapter, you learn social work is never isolated to one thing or event; it all happens at once. These chapters will build on one another until the final chapter.

This will likely be the shortest chapter I have written because I want to raise awareness to the issue, to let you know our clients' homes, bodies, clothes, and even animals will and do smell. If you are sensitive to these things, you might not be the right person in the field social work. Let me discuss geriatrics; if you cannot wipe a person's behind after a blowout, give them a dignified shower. You might be the right person to be a caregiver instead, or you might be better suited for the Activities Director/Assistant. There is nothing that says you cannot talk to your client about hygiene, but if you cannot do it out of love, please do not attempt. These clients have lived so much trauma already, and a social worker should never be the cause of their trauma (child welfare and the like excluded from this statement). We as social workers need to have compassion, and yes, we need to believe that lipstick on a pig can happen. For the record, I am not calling any client a pig; I am using a phrase I am certain Americans have heard and can identify with.

If you know that client XYZ smells from past experiences of being with them, it is okay to carry disinfectant spray in your trunk (do not leave it out for them to see) and use it before your next encounter. In fact, as a courtesy to your next client, try to have thirty minutes between appointments to allow fresh air. It is none of your other clients' business that the previous client smelled. In fact, you might even need that thirty minutes to gain your own composure so you can prepare to work with the next client.

If your client continues to smell, it is not an isolated problem. I would hope compassion will kick in, and you will help your client identify why they are in the state they are in and help move them to a more calm and balanced state. However, like Kim, who I introduced at the start of this presentation, she was not ready to go to the shelter at first. Kim needed to seek services on her terms, and as a result, it was meaningful and beneficial. We as social workers want to solve all the clients' problems, but as discussed earlier, we must not work harder than our clients. If they do not want to change their circumstances, nothing we do will matter. Let's consider a Biblical example. The Prodigal Son got his inheritance, wasted it, and then found himself with the pigs. He came to his senses and realized that his father's servants had it better than him and devised a plan to return to his father, ask for forgiveness, and request to be a servant, certainly not a member of the household. I am confident, at some point, most of your clients will be sick of their situation and will seek your help and graces. When that happens, like Richard, they will realize there are "No Bad Days" and will see the bright side of life. Caution: I warned you earlier, if your client boards the social worker train, you better be ready to get on board with them.

The purpose of this chapter is to highlight that each person you work with is unique; they are human and deserve dignity. It was said early on in my social worker career, "All of us are one paycheck from being on their side of the window," and if you remember that, live humbly and you will accomplish great things. Additionally, if you can understand, our clients, their houses, and their animals will smell and they will want to be treated equally. I cannot write enough, but you will do amazing things as a social worker. If you have not dealt with this side of social services, you have missed some critical situations. If you need time to collect yourself, that is fine. If you are ready to continue onward with the journey, let's go.

Just recently, I met with a supervisor and commented how sad the client's house was—the smell was the worst I have ever encountered as a social worker. I explained that between my previous visits and the last visit, the smell and condition of the home was not humane. The supervisor did not know how to help this person. Because of my background in mental health, I suggested she call the County Pre-Commitment Investigator and have them do a welfare check on this client. Although my training would let me do this, my position and duties did not allow; therefore, I advocated for this client through someone who can help using what I knew to empower this supervisor to make a difference for this client. Yes, her house smells. Yes, it is better than living under a bridge. Yet it is not sanitary or safe. Safety cannot be understated just because it is better than living under a bridge. Let me be clear. If you are judging their situation because it is not your ideal situation, that is wrong; rather, if you are judging it because it is not safe, that is another story.

I will never forget the day a primary worker met me in my office with our mutual client. After the client was dismissed, I engaged in further conversation with the primary worker. "Well, your office was new and nice, smelled nice until *she* came in." Those words hurt me because if that worker has that opinion of this client, how can they possibly help them? I knew my client had hygiene issues. The fact that she is a human needing engagement was greater than her lack of hygiene. The other social worker could not get over the lack of hygiene. Let's be honest, smell, lack of hygiene, general poverty—they all come with our line of work. Most of all, thirty minutes later, my office had aired out and still smelled and looked brand-new, and I wish that caseworker understood that my office had returned to its original state fairly quickly.

In terms of vehicles, if I may suggest, leather or vinyl seats will clean up better. That may seem marginalizing, but cloth seats will store the smells and stains in ways that leather and vinyl will not. It might cost more money for this kind of automobile equipment, yet the benefits and dignity associated with it will pay off. Social work is not cheap; helping people to get out of their ugly situations cost money. Social worker Program Managers must be responsible with their funds, but some expenses are smart and make sense and can be justified if framed correctly. Just as we are teaching our clients hygiene and life skills, we sometimes have to teach our management teams justification for expenses. If you are a Program Manager reading this, please know this writer has a lot of respect for what you do. Your job is not easy, and we as social workers get to have a lot of fun outside of the office while you are attending workshops, meetings, reading spreadsheets, and having to justify every decision we make. Your work is not going unnoticed. Yes, this is the first chapter to thank the Program Manager, but sincerely, we could not do our jobs without you.

While a geriatric provider, Alex was a client who had a colostomy bag, and (s)he would apologize for the smell of the bag. I am using the name Alex because this could apply to anyone in this situation. It was requested to burn incense; however, I explained that would not be necessary any more than apologizing for the smell.

The client cannot help it, and this writer was met by a need they have. I want to challenge all social workers and health-care workers to understand that some smells are due to medical issues, some are due to mental health issues, and some are due to clients not having the means to clean themselves and/or their clothes. If you cannot handle smells, you are surely not ready for any of these lines of work involving direct care / client relations.

How to Interview for a Social Worker Position

This is the chapter I have most looked forward to writing. If you made it through the other chapters, this chapter intends to help you understand the process of interviewing. If are only reading this chapter, please stop. The other chapters have built to this exposé, and there are significant things the other chapters will have taught you. I want to disclose bias again. This chapter is from my experience, and it does not necessarily apply to your experiences. That is why we are unique as humans. I have purposely segmented this chapter for ease of understanding.

Your Résumé

If you have not thought about your résumé, now is the time to think about it. Also, understand, that is only the start. A lot of employers still require an application after you submitted your résumé to them. More to come on that subject. I have made errors on my résumé in the past—never have I put false information because you are accountable for what you put in your résumé, and if you falsify any information, a company can fire you later on the grounds of false information. I have made a résumé for *Social Service Agency A* and forgot that when I was sending to *Social Service Agency B*, I had left the name of *Social Service Agency A* in the second résumé and sent it to the HR recruiter there. It is okay to apply for multiple positions and agencies, but nobody needs to know where you are looking or what positions you are looking for. That is your personal business.

In fact, during the interview process, unless you have a prospect of choosing job offers, you have no need to disclose where else you have interviewed!

There are chronological résumés, and there are relevant work experience résumés. You need to pick a style in most cases. No, you do not need every job you have worked in on your résumé. If you are starting out, just out of college, and/or entering the social service scene, you may have a one-page résumé. Currently, my résumé is three pages because of the experiences I have gained and how I represent those experiences. Let me caution you. S two- or three-page résumé better be necessary because you will not impress seasoned HR recruiters with fluff! If your college or career program has a career adviser, use them. When I did my MBA, the Career Advisor helped me develop my résumé format, and it has been beneficial. Seriously, if you have a Career Center at your college/university, use them; you are paying for it. How can we expect our clients to accept Wrap Around services if we as social workers fail to embrace our own Wrap Around services? Just like I preach about self-care, we cannot expect our clients to take care of themselves if we as social workers fail to do the same!

Become comfortable with the electronic age. I am not here trying to promote one platform over another; however, at the time this is written, LinkedIn, Indeed, and ZipRecruiter are platforms that have been successful in finding jobs, applying for jobs, and gaining an understanding of what kind of employment is available. Furthermore, any internships and/or volunteer opportunities you have enrolled in need to be on your résumé. I cannot discount the impact Craigslist has on finding jobs for yourself (myself included) and your clients as well.

I will caution you. Depending on what kind of job you are applying for, consider *not* putting your full address but rather just the name, city, zip code, and phone number. Employers should treat your résumé like a client's PHI, but you are not guaranteed that protection (unless Congress and your local legislature mandates), and if those protections are in place, you may not know if they will take your PHI as serious as you are required to take your clients' PHI.

Just like you do not want your clients to know where you live, until you get the job, there is no need for your future employer to know where you live! Never put your Social Security number on your résumé and maybe not even on an application. I might add, your ID and/or Driver's License should not be put on a résumé either. That said, if you have a professional license number, maybe put that, but expect that employers might do an initial check on your credentials. Therefore, I cannot stress enough that it is your duty to ensure that your license and/or credentials are updated and renewed in time and on time. When I worked for a skilled nursing home, I saw HR left a note to the CNAs, LPNs, and RNs that it was their responsibility to renew their licenses and allow enough time for them to process, or they would be out of work on their own time.

References do not go on your résumé. When I was in high school, I was taught to put my references on a résumé. Your prospective employer will ask you for them if they find it necessary. Also, this protects your references' information. Instead, ASK for letters of recommendation from volunteers and/or employers. Let me caution you. It is better to have these letters of recommendation before you need them. There are some places that will not accept applications without letters of recommendation. When I attempted to apply at our local Community College, they required a specific number of Letters of RecommendationS in order to even submit your résumé. Also, do not lose them; they are part of your professional portfolio. My letter of recommendation from my previous supervisor and coach/mentor/boss at my high school job is still in my possession, and since my coach/mentor/boss has since passed, that letter is personal and a lasting memory of the impact he had on me.

I will detour a bit. If you have a professional who is leaving, offer to write them a letter of recommendation. I have done this for other professionals as well as for my Speech and Debate students. We as professionals should be in the business of building up another professional. I fundamentally believe in collective success. Unless you are coaching and have a specific advantage that you do not want to give away, make the next professional a rock star.

Set Up Your Voice Mail

I cannot tell you how many people, including clients, miss opportunities because they do not have a voice mail set up. But that is half the battle. Ensure that your voice mail is professional. Currently, my name is not on my voice mail because I am also the voice mail for myself, my disabled father, and a message center for my children. But my message is professional. Do not try to be funny with your voice mail; do not have the sounds of last week's party or loud music. Let's assume you are already a professional, so make your voice mail professional. Yes, I did assume, but I think the chances of making an ass out of you and me is much less in this context!

On your voice mail, it is best to say what number they called. It is possible that they dialed by error. If your name is not listed, at least have a number for them to reference. Now that you have established your voice mail, if you are a professional, check it DAILY. HR recruiters will not wait for you to call back days later; they have made multiple calls to people and will go with a returned call. I cannot tell you how many people I have heard report back to me that their voice mail was a reason why they were not selected. Your voice mail is a statement of your character, and if your first impression is not professional, there will likely be no other second chances.

It drives me crazy when I call another professional, and their voice mail has old dates concerning their absence. If you cannot update your voice mail, how confident am I that you will follow through with the needs of your clients and/or organization? A voice mail that is outdated is a negative statement, and negative statements affect your ethos. That said, you do not need to announce an absence on your personal cell phone unless it also duplicates as a work phone. (Caution: I recommend separating the two phones' purposes.)

Understand, the number that is listed on your voice mail may not be the number to call back; therefore, do not delete your voice mail until you have written down the name of the person calling you and their returned number. When I worked for the community mental health provider, the outgoing number was a dummy number; therefore, you could not call it back and get through. If you want to capitalize on these opportunities, you need to be ready to act. Let me be blunt. If you cannot react fast for your own good, how can you be expected to act fast for clients who need you to act fast? As I have navigated my Dad's acute hospital care, one particular hospital would reply when calling the number back, "You have reached an unestablished extension." Had I not kept the voice mail to know what number to call back, chances are I would be at the mercy of an operator attempting to do their best.

<u>Do Your Research</u>

It was discussed earlier that employers are going to likely check your résumé credentials. They will also look at your social media, so why would you not do the same? No shame in saying, if I know who is going to interview me, I will look them up on social media to see who they are, maybe what their interests are, or what their background is. If they will know something about me, you bet I want to know something about them. I will also do exhaustive searches on their standing in the community, what people are saying about them. Seriously, not all reviews are valid. People get emotional and react when given a platform; therefore, I will read a lot to get an impression. The culture of the workplace can be understood in many respects by the reviews and endorsements of the person(s) you will engage with.

If they are a nonprofit, I may look at their financial statements. Seriously, do you want to work for a company that is not stable? Are they certified by another body? What does the hierarchy of the company look like? If they are a corporation, I will look at their Annual Report. Caution: if you do not have a business degree, this may be difficult to read and understand, but regardless, I will tell you about the culture of the workplace. If you do not nerd for your financial benefit, what makes you believe you will nerd for your clients' benefits?

Workplace culture matters. As an undergraduate, I focused on organizational communication and culture. An organization that is not organized and fails to have a positive culture will be a miserable experience. Yes, you might be able to change the culture—caution: do you think a new person walking into the setting is going to be taken seriously if you attempt to make changes right away? Unless you are the manager, this is not likely going to be a starting point for you. I might add, checking on their status with the credit agencies and/or Better Business Bureau may be good thing to do as well.

When I was a freight broker and I went to work for a new company, this taught me a lot. I will likely never take a position with a start-up company again. But I gained a lot of experiences, and they were willing to train someone who had ambition but not freight broker experience. Therefore, if you need experience, this may be a starting point, but if you are a seasoned professional, you may want to look for established companies. That said, if you know the person who has started up the company and they are solid, respected in the industry, that could change things too. If you have not figured out, I am pleading with you to do your research. If you are not willing to do your research on your next employer, can we trust you will do the research necessary to help your clients (I cannot repeat this enough)? Yes, what you do as a professional will say a lot about what you will do in the role of a professional!

Humbly Take Risks

I had entered paid social services by accident as identified earlier in this presentation. I took a temporary position, and it led to direct hire. I cannot tell you how scared I was to take a temporary position, but I also understood it was the best means of getting my foot in the door. It worked, and I had two tenures of employment with that agency as result of layoffs and turned down a third opportunity because life circumstances had changed. If I did not accept the risks of being a temporary employee, there is no chances of having gotten to where I am today. Social workers must be humble. The work we are doing with our clients is hard. It is demanding, and it is aggravating, but if we remain humble, results will happen. Just like Richard when he got sober, he came to the reality that there are "No Bad Days," and that can be your social service journey as well.

If the church or community organizations you are aligned with hosts a feed the hungry, cloth the poor, and/or other things like this, get involved. You will learn so much, and your clients will benefit beyond words. There is a reason I am writing this now, and I will develop more of that. I cannot stress how important being willing to volunteer is. Let's be honest, all of us work to make money, but if you are only doing good deeds for money, I am afraid that you are entering the wrong profession. Social work is not likely to make you rich (unless you are the executive and even that may not be the case); therefore, volunteer for the greater good and learn skills and services that can be applied in your paid capacities. In case I have scared you against going into social work, understand that once you master entry-level social work, you can return to school, gain your focused graduate degree, and make an advanced difference in your clients' lives.

Social Services and Resources Are a Happy Marriage

I am not in a manager role, but if I was, I can assure I will value how many resources you know, understand, and can connect clients with. I have never spoken in an interview about a resource I am not confident in, but I have spoken about my awareness and acknowledged how to access it is not a point of expertise for me. I do not want to think too highly of myself. A Peer Mentor I worked with commented on my understanding of resources. Before you freak out, it took me years to develop this. You will not master resources overnight or through your college experience; rather, it is by doing.

I am going to challenge you and maybe offend you, and I am okay with both of those. Churches and civic organizations are your friends. If you do not identify with a faith/denomination/faith, that does not mean it is not a valuable resource. Therefore, you must know that to be a successful social service agency, know two food pantries, their dates and times of service, and how to access them. You must also know where the community health center is, what insurances they accept, and if they are accepting new patients. You must also know where the Housing Authority Office is located and its days and time available, and you must know who provides mental health services, followed by at least two substance abuse treatment agencies in your area. Granted, I am writing from the perspective of my communities in Oregon; therefore, two agencies might not be realistic where you reside, but you get my point.

Do you know where the Social Security office for your region is? Do you know where the Medicaid office is? The "food stamps" office is? And do you know where the senior resource center is? How about the Disability Service Office? Did you really think that social services only specialize in one area? Oh my, you would be really lucky to find that, but in most cases, you are going to be asked to cast wide nets of opportunities for your clients. Please do not hoard resource knowledge to make yourself look good! I hope you want to be engaged in social services for the greater good, and part of the greater good is helping other social workers and clients.

I had the pleasure of working with Bill, my first US veteran outside of the skilled nursing home. I disclosed to Bill I have not done social work for veterans, but I will do some nerding to learn and help him navigate the systems necessary. I explained I actually like bureaucracy, and he replied, "You are sick." But clients are seeking our help because they likely do not know where to start or how to access resources. I had talked with another member of my agency what I needed to know about serving veterans and learned of a resource. I went to the place, asked to have a session to talk through this case (I did not have an ROI; therefore, I could only paint a picture but no specific details), and in 30 minutes, I learned three things I never knew and understand how to help this veteran. I was able to meet confidently with a Wrap Around provider to discuss my limitations and became empowered to help my client. As a result, Bill got the services he needed and the navigation that would solve his case, and the next veteran is ready for my assistance.

This may not be normal social work, yet do you know where the skilled nursing homes, the assisted livings, the foster homes are? Do you understand that there are different kinds of foster homes? Yes, there are mental health, developmental disabilities, and senior and adult (and children). But all these have different licensing levels, and some only accept Medicaid, some accept a cap on Medicaid clients, and others only private pay. Therefore, you need to know, do they have a Medicaid contract so a client can age in place, or if that client spends down and will end up on Medicaid, will they need to move into a Medicaid-approved home? If you have never heard of aging in place, this is an important concept I want you to investigate and master.

Do you know who can do notary? This gets into a world you want to be cautious. Anything legal, unless you have a law degree, does not exceed your scope of practice as discussed earlier. But your clients might need to be put in touch, and if you know who is who for these clients, you will save time and capitalize on your client's needs. Let me warn you, NEVER be a witness for your clients—even as a volunteer or a paid social worker. You can find a witness, but this is a risk that you do not want to take. I know earlier I wrote about risks; however, even earlier I wrote about covering your ass, and you will open yourself up to issues if you act as a witness. In most cases, you will not be a single-agent social work, you will be working on behalf of an agency, your actions will influence your agency, and that will likely follow you through the rest of your career.

Do you know where the property management companies are located? Have you researched which might be best for your clients? Some require three times income to rent ratio; others might be less. And if you do not know which require three times versus less, you will not be able to successfully advocate for your clients' housing needs. I have yet to meet a client who has three times the rent; therefore, I will not even go into those property management companies. In fact, most social workers on their own income without a spouse/relationship fail to do this. If you think you will get rich doing social work, you are entering for the wrong reasons! Let me be clear. You should expect insurance and even appreciate some type of retirement plan, and should those benefits be offered, ask yourself, Is the salary they are paying when combined with benefits enough?

In addition to property management companies, do you know what companies/agencies provide and coordinate Transitional Housing? Many of our clients need skills training to become responsible renters and/or lack the money and resources to move into their own place immediately. I am the first to advocate that housing and being off the streets is essential to well-being; nonetheless, getting clients shelter that is not sustainable will not help them. Tour the transitional houses if possible; learn where the Oxford Houses are too. Not all clients need foster care or qualify for foster care, and not all clients will accept the restrictions imposed by missions; therefore, as a social worker, the more housing resources you know, the more equipped you are to advocate for your clients.

Have you ever been to the mission? Yes, your clients might need the mission, but knowing where it is, is not good enough. Many missions have criteria that you must be familiar with: Do they allow smoking? Do they allow clients to work and/or come in late because of work? Do they require being affiliated with a religious institution, and if so, what "religious institution" will they accept that meets this standard? And do they allow children and/or families? I have clients that I cannot send to the mission in my areas because they will not comply with the rules; however, if I was not familiar with these rules, I might refer them to the hope of shelter to learn it is not possible.

Are you aware where the warming shelters are? Do you know what the application and/or screening process is for getting into a warming shelter? If I have created a headache for you, welcome to social services, but once you master these resources, you will be able to universally apply them to your clients. Yes, as discussed earlier, each client is unique, but each social service opportunity will not likely change their criteria to the uniqueness of your clients. During the summertime, if you are in a hot and humid environment, do you know where the places for your clients to cool down are? Let me disclose, I am not writing out of theory; I am aware of all these resources I have written to you, have effectively used them for my clients, and have demonstrated competency in interviews. But I did not learn them in a week or a month; I learned them by referring clients and nerding. As a social worker, you will likely work and not get paid. I spend some of my spare time looking for resources and understanding them. That is not paid by my employer(s). My "spare time" nerding makes me a better social worker. Being a nerd has its benefits, and I would rather have a social worker who is a nerd than an uncompassionate, educated, power-hungry person who cannot see the worth of its clients. Caution: if you want to marginalize our clients, please do not consider social services as our clients have experienced enough trauma without your unnecessary contributions.

Have you ever been in secondhand stores? Do you know where the Salvation Army, St. Vincent de Paul, and other agencies are located? Our clients need all these services. However, if you do not know where they are, what help can you be? I would argue that if you do not know ten resources to present in an interview, how to access all ten if asked, and how to apply them to your clients' needs, you are needing some experience. Volunteer and/or do internships to gain this experience, or do some nerding as discussed earlier.

Do you know where the courthouse is located and the specific courthouse? What! Yes, there are child and juvenile courthouses (in some cases) and adult courthouses. There are Circuit Courts, Municipal Courts, and Federal Courthouses. If you go to the wrong courthouse, depending on your geographic area, you will have wasted time, your client may be held in contempt of court if required to be there, or your client may be late, creating a bench warrant. I write this paragraph from experience. Your clients might not know what courthouse they need to appear, so attempt to learn this before the court date. If you get a subpoena, ensure that the courthouse is the location.

Do you know where the Parole, Probation, and Public Defender's offices are located? Understand, our clients, in many cases, come with legal issues. Do you know where the nonprofit legal aid office is located? I have not used these resources as much, but when you need them, it is not the time to find them. I am urging you to expand your horizons, to understand that social services are exhaustive, but the results of success are rewarding. In all my years of work, my work as a social worker, next to having been a dietary chef, has given me the most warmth and fuzziness out of any career choice.

Let me challenge you. Do something ahead of helping your clients, and you will likely need it too. Do you have a Certified Birth Certificate? Have you ordered a Certified Birth Certificate? Do you know what state and possibly county agency maintains these documents? I will not provide you the answers to this because if you do not know this, you need to immediately learn this because your clients will frequently need a Certified Birth Certificate. In fact, some of your clients might need help ordering a Death Certificate. Do you have the understanding to make this happen? I have referred to nerding earlier, and I want to challenge you to nerd to get these tasks accomplished. It is acceptable for a social worker to not know the answers to your clients' needs, unless it is a task that you will do many times for clients, like ordering a Birth Certificate.

Having raised the questions of ordering Birth Certificates, do you know what the required documents are in your state to apply for an ID and/or a Driver's License? Your clients cannot get a job without government-issued ID and cannot get their Social Security cards without a valid government ID. The catch is, both of these require a Birth Certificate (in the State of Oregon). Should your agency not be an agency that funds these tasks, do you know which social service agencies help pay for these documents? Okay, maybe you know the agencies, but do you know when they are open and if you need to make an orientation appointment or just walk in? The more you know about the process, the better you can maximize your time and your client's time. Also, being prepared like this demonstrates to your clients that you know what you are doing. Being a green social worker is natural; we all start somewhere. The difference is, most agencies expect that by the end of your probationary period, if you are being paid, you are adding value to their clients and the staff. At the end of the day, social work is about doing a good deed and running a well-oiled business.

<u>Identify Your Weakness</u>

It was discussed earlier about your ethos, and in my case, I have not worked much with children social services. I understand some of the series due to my children's disabilities; however, if I was to be a Case Manager for children, I would need to do some nerding and shadow maybe longer than a week, but my skills are universal in how I can use them. Just as discussed earlier in this chapter, before Bill, I had not worked with a US veteran outside of the skilled nursing home. You will not know everything about social services. As a seasoned social service worker, I remember the week I had learned four new things before the end of the week. It made me a better advocate because I was willing to embrace my lack of understanding.

Due to being a parent of multiple children with disabilities, I am familiar with IEPs, but not all IEPs are the same, just like not all disabled children and/or adults qualify for K-Plan benefits. If IEP and K-Plan are foreign terms to you, take time to nerd and determine what agencies you need to contact to coordinate an IEP and/or K-Plan service(s). I will promise you, unless these are your specialties, you should simply navigate your clients to these resources, advocate, and like previous discussions, do not neglect doing proper ROIs. Full disclosure, my wife has coordinated my children's IEPs mostly because I am working during these periods. My client who has Autism receives K-Plan services, and I was only introduced to it because my previous employer managed the K-Plan services or its geographic area residents. Sometimes, what you learn about social services is by accident. Acknowledge what you have no experience, an academic understanding, and an actual understanding; doing so will make you and those you work with better. Lack of understanding is not a failure but rather a chance to professionally grow.

As identified earlier, I have been in recovery since 2005; however, I got clean and sober before having children and a family. Therefore, when my clients are dealing with alcohol and drug issues and are in a relationship and/or have children, I cannot identify with their circumstances, but I am trained to recognize how to help and am compassionate to their situation. I cannot state how important being compassionate is. I also quit smoking in 2005. I will always accommodate a smoker, yet if they want support in quitting, I am all ears as well.

Through my work, I have read Treatment Plans and Care Plans. I have never written a Treatment Plan but have written and amended many Care Plans. Just because you have never done something does not disqualify you; rather, if in the interview you claim you can do something, you best be capable. If you have no experience with a Treatment Plan and/or Care Plan, I urge you to nerd immediately because that will be crucial to being a good social worker. In understanding the scope of practice, you might not be required to write Treatment Plans and/or Care Plans; therefore, just being familiar with and/or understanding how to read them might be good enough. There is not a single geriatrics position and/or clinical social worker position that will not require understanding of one or both of these documents.

If you have never written a clinical note, you need to identify this. That does not disqualify you. Rather, as a Navigator, my notes are not clinical like they were as a Certified QMHA. I am taking credit for the work done and identifying how I have accomplished the goals. Now that leads to the Golden Thread—everything we do in social services should come back to the Golden Thread. The idea of the Golden Thread is what ties all our actions and interactions back to the core needs of the clients identified in the Treatment Plan, Care Plan, and/or referral. If you are doing tasks outside of the scope of what is asked, do them, but document why and remember the referral and its goals and expectations needing to be accomplished. Side work is not like high school extra credit; it is not always a good thing! If you understand the Golden Thread, tell your interview team because this will tell them a lot about you. If you have never heard of it, rest assured, I was more than three years into my work as a social worker before I even heard the term. In fact, it was not until I was on the panel to interview for our supervisor that I had even heard of it. Nonetheless, I understood it.

<u>Watch for Medicaid/Insurance Fraud</u>

Let me first say, if you have ever committed insurance fraud, billing for services not rendered or billing for time not actually used, you are no longer qualified for social services—period! As a Navigator, I did my time just like I did as Certified QMHA, exact time in and exact time out. There is an exception. If I get a message, call, or voice mail from a client while with another, I will document that encounter at a different time but will note the change of time and only document the time that took. There is nothing wrong with that because I cannot help two clients at once, with the exception of groups, and to this discussion, talk with your agency on how groups and billings work.

Please do not be afraid to charge for your services. I work with a CADC (Certified Drug and Alcohol Counselor) that considers how each task can be billed because money is important to running the organization and getting yourself paid. I also watched a credentialed QMHA whom I worked with get fired for Medicaid fraud. This person damaged our profession and the organization, and the client who reported the fraud was affected because they learned they could not trust that person and wondered if every other social worker would be the same. I am going to keep this segment short because I believe social workers are professionals and do their best to be rock stars, yet there are a few rogue agents. And if you do not think insurance fraud will be found, good organizations have officers doing checks to ensure that there are no issues because they would rather self-audit than be audited by an actual governing body.

<u>Your Personal E-mail versus Social Work E-mail</u>

You should always use your personal e-mail to apply for other jobs and inquire on positions. Your current employer or agency expects their e-mail to be used for official business. In fact, depending on where your organization gets its funding, nonwork use of e-mail could be fraud. You should always use your social service e-mail to send to referral agencies and community providers. If it does not contain PHI, you can forward it to your personal e-mail if it is something you want to have a record of, but e-mail is a tool that should be professional. E-mail will either enhance your career or leave you looking for a new job.

Speaking of professional, is your e-mail address professional? Just like what is discussed about voice mail earlier in this segment, your screen name and e-mail address should not create questions about you. If you are sharing an e-mail with spouse/relationship, do not conduct career and/or professional business with it because you need to represent yourself. Your "hip" middle school / high school screen name might need some adulting if you expect to be taken seriously as a professional. Seriously, I have learned of more candidates disqualified because of a childish e-mail.

In terms of your social worker e-mail, have an end script containing your name, title/credentials, address or geographic location, whom you are working/volunteering for, and phone number to reach you. Also, if you are doing alcohol and drugs, ensure that you notify receipt of the requirements associated with the 42 CFR Part 2 and maybe a statement of HIPAA. If you are going to be out of reach, use an "away" message that is professional and shows how to triage the need to contact you if urgent and when you expect to return.

E-mails will get you in trouble. I know that we are talking about the interview process, but if you e-mail the person interviewing you, look to see if others are on the e-mail. Just like discussed earlier about the hazards of *REPLY ALL*, determine if you need to use *REPLY ALL* to ensure everyone knows that you will accept the interview. Another tip is, verify the location of the interview. Just because Company XZY is doing the interview does not mean you will be doing an interview at their office. I had been interviewed for a management position at a bank's conference room because that was where the interview team requested; showing up at the place of employment might have alerted people who do not need to know interviews were being done or have disrupted the flow of work, and like the court examples, it would have made me late for the interview.

<u>Dress to Impress</u>

I am writing as the male sex that identifies a male and ask that you read this understanding that. Unlike how you dress with your clients, it is okay to dress up for an interview. But be comfortable. You do not know if the room will be cold or hot. Therefore, you do not want to show up cold or sweating from wearing a wool jacket. You get the point. Make sure your socks are the same color and they match; nothing like thinking those were both blue socks to find out one is black and the other is blue.

If you do not iron, make sure your shirt and slacks are not wrinkled. Put it through the dryer at least if necessary. Never wear stained clothes to an interview. But like working with your clients, leave the powder, cologne, and lotions at home. You do not want to smell like a spa, but you do not want to smell like a locker room either. From personal experience, if you know your interview is on Tuesday, get your hair cut by Saturday because your hair might need a few days to cooperate after getting cut. I might add, if you know where the interview is being held, scope it out, determine how long it takes to get there, see what the parking is like, etc.

You can wear comfortable shoes or formal shoes, but make sure they do not contradict your presentation. If you have a briefcase, do not bring it unless they have asked you to bring a portfolio. Again, you are not trying to oversell yourself. We have a saying in social services, "Underpromise and overdeliver." The same can be said about you. You do not want to advertise you can do something and not be capable. You do not want to dress like you are seeking management when you are seeking a housing advocate or victim's advocate position. It is a delicate balance.

There is never a good reason to wear clothes with holes in an interview or once hired. What you wear on your spare time is fine, but you should be a higher standard than that. Like the state worker who was wearing a beer company beanie, just do not do it. Gentleman, I wear facial hair. If you are going to an interview (my personal thoughts here), make sure your mustache, goatee, and/or beard is kempt. I do not want to offend anyone, but you are not seeking a job as a laborer; you are seeking a job as a professional. You need to look like it (I have nothing against laborers).

I have been accused as a Speech and Debate Coach and Judge as being the fashion police. It is because dress affects ethos. You do not want to dress in ways that create unnecessary power statements. I might add, if you are applying for an entry-level position, a two-hundred-dollar suit is not realistic; you will create questions as to why you are dressed so expensive compared to the rate you will be paid. If you cannot tell, employability is a lesson in psychology.

Be Open-Minded

I will go into further discussion about this in another chapter, but understand, your assumptions, dogmas, and lifestyles are going to be challenged if you enter into social work. You do not have to identify with the drug and alcohol client or the dual-diagnosis client (those with mental health and substance abuse disorders), nor do you have to love sex offenders, but you have to know, these are snapshots of your clients. Be compassionate! You will work with users, abusers, those who have faced trauma, or those who are in transition and/or questioning their sex and/or sexuality. There is not an "ideal" client; you are not marrying and/or dating them; therefore, be ready to meet them where they are and accept their baggage.

I might offend you; however, your belief systems should be that—yours and not unfairly applied to your clients. If you cannot do this, I will request you to not be a social worker but maybe a support staff member. If that last statement offends you, I stand by it and validate your offense. By validating your offense and/or validating your clients' experiences, that is the start of being open-minded. I can promise you, you will not like every client you come in contact with; you might even be mortified by their behavior. That is natural and okay. I just want you to accept them as a fellow human. Being compassionate is necessary. I will never agree with a sex offender, but my lack of agreement does not mean I cannot help them better their circumstances. Seriously, we are human; we have biases. Just be ready to identify them and help them move forward.

Leave Your Current Position and Start a New Position as a Professional

Unless your current situation is illegal and/or unethical, there is not much justification for less than two weeks' notice and maybe even a month's notice in some cases. I cannot stress how important being a professional to your current employer and to a new employer is. In my work experience, I have only left one employer with no notice. I was a Medication Aide and went from overtime to reduced hours, making me nearly homeless. I was offered a job and accepted immediately because I had to support my family and not be homeless.

In other words, if you were interviewed, accepted a job as a part-time, and found a full-time position, you owe it to yourself and your employer to give proper notice before advancing to a full-time position. Social workers are not easy to replace; our jobs are plentiful, but we specialize in specific aspects of social work or bring specific skills that replacing your services is difficult. Just because we have the same titles does not mean the way we do the job is not always the same. As a Certified QMHA, I was working with clients to teach them medication compliance, how to shop, create budgets, maintain housing, empower them to cook better, and basic life skills. I was then invited back to write Care Plans and assist with the management of Transitional Housing. My title did not change, but the job did, and I was hired because I had the specific skills necessary to write Care Plans and manage the daily affairs of Transitional Housing.

If you need to negotiate time off necessary during your probationary period, be up front about it. I have never met an employer who wanted to hire me but rejected prescheduled commitments. That said, I had to be flexible in how I was going to make these precommitments work, but communication is key to social work. Your Program Managers and Executive Managers will help you if they understand where you need help. That does not mean they will understand your job. They hired you as the professional; they are your managers, but you are the mover and shaker for your clients.

You were hired because you understand resources, how to access them, how to execute the Treatment Plan / Care Plan, and maybe even write them. Management was hired because they understand how to manage the daily affairs. They might have done social work in the field, but it might have been years ago. Do not be arrogant and believe you have something over your manager; they control your ability to get a paycheck and maybe unemployment if terminated!

When you choose to leave a company, agency, and/or service, do not burn your bridges. To this day, I maintain contacts with my geriatric, community providers, and agency referral sources. It is okay to be friends and/or professional acquaintances with these individuals. If you bash your employer and/or referral agencies on social media, it will haunt you. Just like you are leaving a job one day to enter a new job, the person you bashed might have become the manager or your future coworker where you want to work next. The world is a small place, the United States is a small place, and your local community is even smaller. It is in your ability to create a fool of yourself. That said, you can have differences of opinion and thought. Just like our clients are unique, you are unique as well. Just do not make your agenda your client's agenda.

Hardly will you agree with all your coworkers; rather, what can you learn from them? Seriously, there should not be a one-person show—ever! No social worker is so amazing that they cannot learn something from another staff member. Be humble. Just because you have a degree (if you do) and have credentials and/or certifications/ licenses, this does not mean your coworkers are not keys to your success. Remember, that week that I learned multiple things before Friday, it was because I was humble that it was possible. Your Office Manager, Office Assistant, IT, Compliance Officer, Mail Clerk, Maintenance Worker, Fleet Manager, etc., they all make your job possible. Treat them all like the professional you believe you are. If you think you are better than the custodian, please save all of us from your heightened sense of self!

<u>Drama Isn't Productive</u>

If I need to remind you that workplace and other unnecessary drama is not needed, you are in bad shape already. In fact, your coworkers do not have to be your friends just like your clients are not your friends. But you must be friendly, compassionate, and professional. If you hear a rumor about another agency from other social workers, investigate it (this is where being a nerd happens) and determine if it might be valid. If there is drama in the office, take the high road and avoid it.

Social workers should be too busy for needless drama. If you have time to participate in workplace drama, your notes should be completed; otherwise, you are being counterproductive. Let me warn you. Your e-mails and phone calls might be monitored; therefore, watch yourself. I do not want you to justify being two-faced, but understand, your actions are karma associated.

We discussed earlier about ROIs, and I hope you now understand that ROIs will control drama. If you cannot discuss or engage in something because failure to have obtained the proper release of information, you will be relieved from being a victim or perpetrator of this nonsense. I have spent much time in this exposé to explain that you are a professional. Amateurs engage in mindless drama and destroying others' character.

<u>It's Not My Job</u>

If you feel this way, I say this, please do not bother being on my team! That said, if it is not in your scope of practice or you are not qualified, that is understandable. I have no respect for the office person who is too good to clean the toilets and/or take out the trash but is willing to drive the car to get fuel. The sexiest tasks in the office are always going to have a volunteer. Be a team player and step up for the unattractive tasks. I am not going to write much about this because I want to believe people I work with are professionals, yet I have also worked long enough to know this is not the case. If you are not going to be part of the solution/success, please get out of the way of the those doing the work.

Also, just because you are qualified to do something does not mean it is proper for you. Division of labor is important in a well-oiled workplace. If you want to help and you know it is your duty, ask if you can help. That said, I doubt any Program Manager will mind you vacuuming the lobby and taking out the trash or cleaning the bathroom (if your notes are done and finalized). Reread that last statement. Your notes are how you take credit for the work you were hired to do; the other work is what makes for a successful office. Do not forget that you were hired for a task.

I am going to make a short detour. Before you speak to the media about your job and/or company, get clearance from your management team. There are likely standards in place for media relations, and you can quickly disqualify yourself by overstepping your occupational boundaries. In fact, if you do not know the media policy, do not worry about it. Find out and verify EACH TIME you might need to know it because change in organizations happen, and you do not want to be on the wrong side of an old policy. Ignorance in social work is no defense; as professionals, we are held to a high standard.

Final Thoughts on This Chapter

Please learn your scope of practice and operate in that area and appreciate divisions of labor. I touched on that in the previous segment, but social workers are well-meaning people, and that desire to do good can get us in trouble. Understand the limits of your license, certification, and/or job description. When I was chef in training at my undergraduate institution, one of the chefs I worked under told me, "Matthew, the only stupid question is the one you don't ask." That has guided me as a professional. I may not always know what my question is, so I will ask my Program Manager if I can frame the problem and have them help me understand what my question is.

If you police yourself, the need for others to do so will be limited. Social workers must be capable of working independently and be trusted with that fact. I have never been micromanaged as a social worker because I do my job with integrity. Your calendar is not yours; it is the property of your agency as they pay you based on that calendar. If you are in an entry-level position, expect more Supervision and demand for answers; if you are intermediate to advanced (I do not mean your education but actual experience), you will have less need to be under Supervision but given the keys to the business to make things happen.

Know your company's overtime policies. Most social workers outside of child welfare and senior services will not allow for overtime or will ask you to flex the week to be in your assigned hours. I will admit, I have put my own time in for a client, but in most cases, it is because I am nerding to determine what I need to know about helping that client. I do not expect my employer to pay me for my desire to understand something beyond my forty-hour week ability to learn it.

Have fun! When I Coach Speech and Debate, my first practice is telling my students that they must have fun, or it is not worth doing. Failure to enjoy your job will make you, your clients, and your coworkers miserable. An unhappy and/or negative social worker should find a job better suited for them. A social worker who lacks empathy and compassion should not apply. A social worker who has their own agenda at the expense of their employer and/or clients is doing damage.

"I Hate Country, Rap, and/ or Opera"... Get Over It!

Before you laugh, this conversation is something I have lived and have been angered by. Personally, I do not appreciate country music (I love Western and bluegrass), do not find much merit in rap, and my displaced eardrums cannot appreciate opera. What I do love is Southern gospel and worship music, soft rock, and most of the Top 40 songs currently playing. Yet when a client gets into my social worker vehicle or comes into my office, my personal preferences are secondary.

I will automatically turn off my Christian-style music because I am not being paid to make followers of Christ. On a personal note, yes, I would hope everyone would come to find Salvation and live in Heaven as I believe we can have at the end of life. But not all my clients are going to want to hear about faith or even share my interpretation of faith. Therefore, it would be wrong for me to subject them to the hostilities of my music. Just like I make sure clients who want to consider the Mission understand that they will have to accept the rules of the Mission, it is a client's responsibility to accept those rules, but it should not be a client's responsibility to accept my music preferences to get my help. That said, if a client puts on Christian radio, I may engage in a friendly conversation about faith, but this is not an opportunity to preach and/or persuade them to your specific dogma.

I want to discuss rap music. If clients get in my car and put on rap music, I will allow it. But if the language becomes offensive or demeaning to women, minorities, etc., I will kindly ask for them to change the station, or it will be turned off. At that point, the client was given a choice, but it would be inappropriate to just turn off the radio. If they ask what I want to listen to, I may suggest. The point I am trying to make is, clients are in the focus. A client who is not comfortable with the social worker's presence and setting will not get the best offered to them.

Let's discuss opera from my perspective. I have an actual disability, and this type of music is painful to my hearing. It would be appropriate to say my disability does not allow this style of music, but it would be wrong to say, "I don't like it. Therefore, you cannot listen to it." If you act like a professional, present the issue like a professional, and I promise you, amazing things will happen.

In terms of the office, your music choices should not interfere with your work and/or coworkers. It should be a background allowing a person like myself to remain focused. It should be appropriate to the office setting. I fundamentally believe rap music is not appropriate for social services agencies and/or your cars if your clients are not the ones putting it on. The words and implications associated with this style of music goes against many of the things we social workers are trying to combat. It will be for you to determine and/or your Program Manager, but that is my belief.

To my volunteer agents and churches/organizations of religious associations, having religious music playing is appropriate. The previous statements were directed more to the secular organizations and providers of nonreligious institutions' social services. Anyone walking in a house of worship for assistance should understand where they are walking into and appreciate that fact. Social workers, prepare your clients if getting services from a religious-based institution that (1) the mood may be different than they expect, (2) clients may be restricted from smoking on the property, (3) language choices may need to be checked, and (4) they may be offered to be prayed for and/or given an invite for church services. If that is too much for your clients (again, if you know your resources and what to expect, you will know if any of those four things are true), then you allow your clients to choose to not receive services there and go without what they could have had while identifying it was their choice. Notice, you want to document that it was the client's choice to reject available services. Oh my, you thought we discussed documentation in full. You see, documentation is never a completed discussion in social work. Sometimes, getting to the Golden Thread is not possible because the client is not willing to embrace what is necessary to solve their case. Question, Are you working harder on solving it than they are?

This chapter was about music choices, yet we got into the weeds of what social work can be. This demonstrates that social work is all-inclusive, the issues faced by our clients are fluid, and the areas of discussion have overlapped. I hope you have read the whole journey instead of just a chapter that interests you because we, through these chapters, like any academic course, are building on previous concepts, and failure to read the whole story will cause confusion.

In my work, Ashley was assigned to my caseload. There were issues of domestic violence, being deemed powerless. When Ashley was transported, she was told, "The radio is yours. Feel free to change the station. However, if the music or words is offensive, I will change, but that will be the only reason." And Ashley said she could benefit from being exposed to other music. Later in the drive, it was a bit hot and humid in the area, so I rolled down the window and explained, "Like the radio, the window is yours too. Therefore, if you need air, roll it down." "Ashley" reported, "I am not used to being told I have control over something." I want to challenge all social workers, coaches, teachers, and such, be prepared to be shocked when a client reports the simple acts of changing the radio and rolling down a window give them power they never knew they had. Just like eating a pizza is changed, now rolling down a window and changing the radio are no longer small things for my life.

I want to address one last thing. The final topic of this chapter's title contains "Get Over It," and it is necessary for social workers to have thick skin. In my years of social work, what causes the greatest turnover is that social workers are not prepared for the realities that we see and are reminded of their own traumas, and sadly, some just want a paycheck and are void of compassion. Not a single social worker can be effective if they are too full of themselves and not focused on the clients. If you cannot distance yourself from your clients' crisis, you will not succeed. I understand that last statement may be applied to myself writing this. This presentation is from my years of experience and cautions and advice, wanting to empower the next social worker.

I want to impress upon you, yes, opera is not my type of music. Had it been any other reason than it hurting my ears based on my disability, I would get over it just as I am asking you. If you cannot deal with the fact that your clients have a right to listen to what makes them feel comfortable, I ask you, Are you going to be capable of doing other acts that will help them relax and be comfortable? This chapter, like many others, is about asking you to take inventory of your biases and assumptions in ways that enhance how you will engage with your clients.

Failure to address and check your biases will have a negative impact on your successes as a social worker. Please understand, music, I believe, is good for the soul, yet what is good for your soul may be unique to you and not universal to your clients. If the music is sexist, gives hint of criminal elements, and/or is offensive in language, I do believe it is my right and responsibility to ask my client to change it and/or totally remove the medium.

Self-Care

If your employer grants you vacation, please use it. If the job you are applying for does not value the fact that you deserve vacation, do not accept it! No, you do not have to use all your vacation, but you need a break. Getting a new perspective is critical to being able to help your clients. None of the employers I have worked for allow Mental Health Days, and as a person with a mental health disorder, I have never taken a Mental Health Day. Instead, I have taken time off with pay to get recharged. If you are sick, especially contagious, you must use your sick time because your clients and coworkers do not need to get sick because of your actions. I met with a QMHP, and she had argued that everyone on their staff takes a Mental Health Day and cautioned me—actually, preached—that failure to do so would cause me to "burn out," but I do not agree. That is what vacation days are used for. My organization and clients deserve this social worker to be engaged, and my self-care becomes my own mandate. If this offends you, this is my own opinion, and after these many years of paid social work experience, I have found it to be true.

Lunch periods and breaks are not optional. If you cannot accomplish the tasks in eight hours with a proper lunch/two breaks, you are doing too much or not efficiently enough (seriously, there are some limited exceptions that come up, but it should not be the norm). If you have the option of working four ten-hour shifts, use that three days off to your advantage. Yes, you will work through a few breaks and lunches—I have done it; it should never be the rule. If you are a smoker, please do not smoke outside of your breaks and lunch because that is unfair to your coworkers who do not smoke. When I was a smoker, I never took a smoke break because I believe in everyone being fair and equitable with their use of breaks.

There are things that social workers can do that do not involve vacation time use. Ladies, I do not have experience with this as a born male, identifying as a male, yet getting your hair done, maybe your nails done, or going for a general spa treatment will rejuvenate you. Men, maybe a coffee break with your friends, workout at the gym, or an outdoors adventure (please understand, women can do all those things too) will recharge you. For me, I like to go on a drive, a hike, fishing, crabbing, attend a political event that fits my persuasions, go to church, participate in family activities, attend a hockey game, window-shop at the mall, watch my favorite TV show with my wife (going on dates with your spouse and/or person you want to date is important), and I love to cook a meal.

In other words, whatever you can do that is *not* work, that does not involve taking your work phone (unless you are required to keep it on you as result of being on call), and to have fun, that is important. I want to challenge you, find ways to recharge that do not require money or lots of money because you can then share those things with your clients who are likely on less money/resources than you. If your whole life is work and no fun, you will be miserable, will burn out, and will become ineffective as a social worker. Just recently, social media informed me of a chili cookout that was going to happen on a weekday after work. I set an early alarm, got up, started my chili, and competed—yes, I started my day early, but it was not starting early for work but rather for something that was fun and exciting.

Never in my years of social work have I been burned out. I have been exhausted—I keep from being burned out because of self-care. Your manager can help you with self-care if you need; make that part of your Supervision. I promise you, failure to take care of yourself means you cannot take care of your clients. If you are burned out, you will not be of any use to your clients. If your company is shut down for a Holiday and you are not required to work that Holiday, please avoid the office. I promise you, it will be there when you return. I remember my Pastor telling us that he is off on Fridays and holds that boundary unless there's a reasonable reason to violate it. It is okay and necessary to take care of yourself because without that, you cannot take care of your clients.

We have not discussed this next concept: delegate. Seriously, you do not have to do it all on your own. Caution: do not create a HIPAA and/or 42 CFR Part 2 violation, but feel free to ask for others to help you. Maybe you need to send faxes but do not have time to send the faxes. If someone is cleared to see that information and they are willing and capable of helping, delegate to them. Maybe, as discussed earlier, the sexy task is refueling the car, but you really need to get that note made, so ask someone to fuel the car for you that is driver cleared and available. If you are a manager reading this, as an undergraduate, I worked for a manager who would not delegate anything because that manager felt like it would threaten their job and status. Do not be so full of yourself to believe that. Empower others to be part of the solution.

The biggest regret I have taking care of my Father's needs is, I have not been able to properly delegate. My parents are divorced. Both of my Dad's parents have died, and the other family is either not equipped or does not want to become equipped; therefore, his affairs have fallen on me to advocate and represent. I can assure you, if it was possible to delegate, I would, because caring for your elderly and/or disabled family is exhaustive.

Life is short. Our clients' problems will still be there. You do not have to solve it at once. Please take care of yourself. It is not your company's fault if you allow them to take advantage of you. We are adults and professionals, and that means we have to fight for ourselves. If labor laws are being violated, report it just like you would report health and safety issues about your clients. On the same token, should you be the cause of labor laws being broken, that is your fault, and you need to correct it immediately. Just like we should not be the tool of ICE and/or the District Attorney, it is not your job to throw your coworkers under the HR bus unless they are violating their oath and credentials or engaging in illegal activities. That will create negative culture and hostilities.

What you do for self-care must be in accordance to your license and/or certification. If you are not in drug and alcohol counseling and/or a Certified Peer Mentor, you may have an adult beverage, but you may not drive with consumption of that beverage. A DUII will negatively affect your employment and future employment. If you are a CADC and/or a Certified Peer Mentor, do not even risk your credentials and reputation for an adult beverage (or fruit cake during the holidays—please know this observation is a serious observation). An employer I worked for required all disclosed employees who are in recovery to remain sober, and if you failed to remain sober, it is recommended you disclose the need for help before HR finds out.

I hope you understand, your recharge is your responsibility. If you expect your clients to do well for themselves, you must also do the things that are well for you. That means proper diet. I am not the diet police here, but if you only eat processed foods or fast foods, skip too many meals, or lack fruits and vegetables and lack a proper mix of proteins, you will never be well. Save your sick time because you are ill, not because your diet made you sick. Social workers are good at "Doing what I say, not what I do," and clients need to know that you are genuine to yourself as well as the message you give them. I am the first to report that I have bought a full-size pizza and ate it on my lunch because I wanted it. There is no shame, but if that is your daily routine, what example are you living for your clients?

I am okay admitting, to date, I have been to a Mental Health Crisis Therapist in a professional capacity twice. The first time, the QMHP confided that they also see a therapist because of the trauma they experienced with clients and their own lives. It is okay to seek professional help; just because you are a professional does not mean you should neglect yourself. I would venture to argue that most doctors and licensed prescribers also get yearly labs and annual checkups for the same reason. You cannot ask your clients to seek help if you are not willing to embrace the same way of life. Due to my life's trauma that brought me the second time, I had to go back to the manager of the day and explained, "I have no further appointments on the calendar today. I am not in a good state of mind to help anyone and/or write my notes. I need to take the rest of the day off." And that was an appropriate use of my sick time because I had lost my ability to function.

Only you can prevent a burnout! If after these many years I have remained burnout-free, I know it is possible. I reported earlier, exhaustion has happened. In fact, most of the time, it is because I have not practiced my self-care but have gone through the motions of self-care. Let's consider this. If you are going on vacation, try to have a day back home before returning to work or a day before you leave on vacation to be prepared for that. A vacation wasted (did not recharge you) is money not well spent—so says me. That said, funerals are not likely to recharge you!

It is okay to remind another professional to take their breaks or take their lunch. We should look out for one another. I remember when I did staffing with another social worker, and it was nearly lunchtime. She knew how busy I was that day, so she said, "Matthew, go take your lunch." And sincerely, I did need to hear that. Yes, eventually, I would have taken my lunch; it is likely my lunch would have been on the go. Let me caution you. If you are eating out every day, it is not good for your health. Pack snacks and meals that will not go bad, or at least find a means to keep cool; you do not want to give yourself food poisoning. Financially speaking, it is not sustainable to eat out each day, and if you create your own budget and learn to budget, you will be even more effective with your clients and in teaching them to budget.

When I first became a credentialed QMHA, not long into that process, I had contracted Shingles. As noted earlier, I have never taken a Mental Health Day. As result, I had sick time necessary to cover my time off. Something made me go to the walk-in clinic, and the physician looked at me and said, "You got Shingles. What do you do for work?" I told him, and he replied, "Not for the next ten days." If I failed to care for myself and had a lifestyle that would make me sick, I would not have had the necessary sick time to pay for my time off. I have known social workers who go to interview for jobs using sick time; that is your ethos at risk. We as coworkers know better. Again, not our job to go to the HR Police, but my respect for them is diminished. Take nothing away from this chapter other than self-care is all your responsibility, and you cannot be a rock star social worker, geriatric provider, coach, clergy, Sunday School worker, volunteer, intern, student, or advocate to your loved one if you fail to do this. To the college students, when you are between terms, try not to intern if possible and recharge so you can become the rock star you intend to be.

Please understand, self-care is not an option. As discussed in a previous chapter, make sure your self-care is in accordance with how it is being paid for. I am not asking you not to travel, not to have fun; rather, in that previous chapter, I was asking you to think about what message it sends. This chapter, I am asking you to think about the message it sends if you do not take care of yourself. Our clients' needs will never go away; your ability to meet them will be diminished if you fail to act on your own behalf. In fact, by doing self-care, you can help your clients be educated on how to budget for their own self-care needs. Again, what we do in our personal lives should have some application to our professional lives.

Failure to do my own self-care disqualifies me from being my Dad's advocate and from being the husband and father my wife and children need me to be. Much of the self-care I engage does not cost me money. Some of the self-care activities require some one-time expense, such as camping for a lifetime of fun. One of my most memorable moments was my wife making a reservation for my oldest and me to go camping together. That night, I spoke with him on a level that I had never done, learned a lot about him, and had a blast. We did not travel very far, did not spend much, but the time was relaxing and recharging.

I want to challenge clients, family, and readers to know hospice is not only about the dying person; rather, hospice is also about the family who remains to get the care and dignity afforded to them. If your first thought that hospice is death, I assure you, hospice can be the most beautiful form of social work/geriatrics.

I will discuss in another chapter about Parenting Your Parents. My late maternal Grandma regretted the lack of self-care she gave herself in the name of caring for Great-Grandma. She loved her Mom but had a false mandate and understanding of what this meant. You will never be effective long-term if you do not slow down and appreciate life and relaxation. You do not owe your boss, coworkers, or clients an explanation for approved time off! That said, ensure that your work can handle your time off or be ready to delegate tasks to a qualified person.

"But *That* Violates My..."

As social workers, you need to be flexible and to leave your dogmas in the parking lot. Do not even bring them into the door of the building or your office. Your clients are unique just like you are. Unless you are working for a dogmatic organization, such as a religious-based institution, you are out of bounds by putting those values and beliefs in practice of your clients' needs/care. I am not asking you to deny yourself, deny your faith, or deny your convictions; rather, I am asking you to take inventory and ask yourself if you can do what is necessary for your clients. Frequently, I will ask you to identify your biases, and if you have yet to do that, pause, do so, then continue to read. The biases you have on social media should not affect your professional abilities.

Planned Parenthood does amazing things for our clients. You do not have to agree with them to take your client. Let's go to the extreme. Your client is recommended to have or wants an abortion, and you have been tasked with navigating them through the process. You can take your client to the appointment, but you are not required to attend the appointment or even go into the office. But to let your personal beliefs deny them a service would be wrong. As a pro-life, born-again Christian and ally of the LBGTQ movement, I can maintain my own value system for myself and empower my clients to do what they need to do. Soon we will discuss Wrap Around services that may help with this problem. That said, I will not participate in a juvenile seeking an abortion without parental/guardian awareness unless it is a case of known incest, because just as I cannot give my Speech and Debate students an over-the-counter medication for a headache, what makes me believe I can take a juvenile for surgery without some kind of authorization? Let me clarify. It is not my religious and/or pro-life views; rather, it is my belief that some aspects of social work are necessary to coordinate with the courts and/or legal authorities.

There are many churches that are working hard to change people's lives. You do not have to attend that church; you can be an atheist/agnostic and still use this service for your clients. Show me a client who deserves to be hungry, cold, homeless, unmedicated, and I will show you a social worker (and/or agency) who lacks compassion. Yet it is reasonable to have a personal belief system that people's choices lead to the above consequences. At the same time, our clients do not need to be reminded of their choices any more than they need to be reminded of their disabilities. It is acceptable to discuss how their choices created barriers; address the barriers, and you will start to address the choices—trust me on this. Clients like Richard and Kim had their barriers identified, and once they accepted those barriers were true, we addressed what caused those barriers. It is vital to address these barriers without judgment. Some of our clients are voluntarily seeking our services, others are Court ordered/committed, and others whose family members are seeking our help to empower the family member to provide for their loved one.

Let's address something important. Just because you would not live *there* does not mean it is not the right place for your client. Kim was living under a bridge, was accepted into the crisis shelter, and then found housing. If I as a social worker had blinders on what was best or sustainable for Kim, no positive outcome would have come. Your life is not the life of your clients, your choices are not the choices of your clients, and your moral compass is not the moral compass of your clients. Leave your dogma as asked earlier in your car. If you transport clients in your car as a volunteer or approved by your agency, leave them at your house. In other words, marginalization of our clients is not your job.

If you are, for example, Catholic or opposed to birth control or have a dogma that sex outside of marriage is morally wrong, live that for yourself. However, our clients need access to birth controls, condoms, and assistance with accessing safe sex practices. It is not likely you are going to Hell because you took your client for birth control (men included), helped them secure condoms, or gave them tips for safe sex. This goes back to my earlier writing about compassion; we as social workers need to do what is best for the client and understand it might be what we would do. The same will apply when we discuss needle exchanges and bring clients to Medicated-Assisted Treatment.

Are you opposed to drug use? Our clients use drugs (not all of them), and some of them need help getting to the needle exchanges and/or methadone clinics / Medicated-Assisted Treatment. You do not have to want that for your life, but for our clients, having someone who sees them as a human who has a drug disease (yes, I believe drug use is a disease, and no, I will not apologize for that) instead of a waste of humanity is necessary. Believe in your clients, get them the help they need, and you will be amazed by the differences you will see in people's lives. Start looking at the drug user who has this disease as equal to the client who has diabetes or any other type of disorder. I never met a drug user who woke up and believed being a junky or getting high was their destination in life. I do not know from experience, but my clients and colleagues tell me that the sickness brought on by not being high is disabling. If you believe letting your client remain physically sick, left out in the cold, and their original choices be lived with the consequences, I assure you, you are not equipped for social services and people will further question your compassion. This is my fundamental issue with my pro-life friends. How can we be pro-life when it is in the womb but so vicious when it is a born human? Being pro-birth without living the principles of being pro-life are counterproductive!

Just a bit ago, I discussed needle exchanges. If you have a problem with drug users being given access to clean and new needles, it may be best to coordinate with another member of the staff or agency to get them there. Yet as a social worker, if you know they are using IV drugs, the greater good of the community and your client should be your mission. As discussed in the chapter "How to Interview for a Social Worker Position," I had hammered hard about knowing as many resources and how to access them. Knowing where condoms for safe sex (and to help prevent the spread of unnecessary infections throughout the community) and where the needle exchanges are is vital to your clients. Also, knowing where the Medicated-Assisted Treatment facilities are, what their operating hours, and how to access them is equally vital to your clients. If you believe a person should not be on Medicated-Assisted Treatment long-term, that is natural, yet it is not appropriate to express that judgment to your client(s). I am not asking you to deny your convictions and biases but rather identify them and keep them to yourself.

I am going to ruffle feathers again (maybe). I am convinced that gender is fluid and not defined. Yes, you are born a sex, and yes, you can change that sex. You can also create a gender identity that matches you. If that offends you, ask yourself, How is a transsexual/transgender person affecting me? More so, how is a homosexual and/or a bisexual affecting me? If these identities have a negative effect on you, I suggest going into social services associated with your specific faith and/or persuasion, but not government, community health, public education, etc. Seriously, if your approach is going to create further trauma to clients, you are not suited for this work.

If you feel attacked by this chapter, I still value you, respect you (likely disagree with you), but it is my journey in social work, life experiences, and academia that have led to this chapter. It is my personal, academic, and spiritual beliefs that cause me to write this. This chapter is based on real-world experiences—my own and those of my clients. You are not being asked to compromise your sincerely held beliefs; rather, you are being asked to advocate and navigate the services needed for your clients. I must stress, you don't have to agree with the behavior; just do not marginalize the clients.

Here's a thought. If you cannot, out of conscience, do something, utilize Wrap Around services. If you cannot help someone to access an abortion, condoms, or Medicated-Assisted Treatment, find a means of helping your client gain these services. Tell your client that you cannot do something (no need to say why), do research on who can help them, put them in touch with the referral source (ROIs come into play here again), and ensure that the clients' needs are being met. To my male social workers, if you are being asked to get female care for your clients and you are not feeling good about that, ask a female staff member to help or utilize Wrap Around services to get the job done. Where there is a will, there will be a way. I am pleading with you, do not let your dogma, values, and/or morals deny your clients' equal access.

Let me speak to the men quickly. If you are being asked to provide a service that is specific to biological and/or transsexual females, do it with a servant's and a professional heart. If you feel you are being asked to do something that violates your conscience, that is fine. Just, in return, ensure that you make provisions for your clients to get that help. I will later tell the story of an elderly resident being given her first shower by a male caregiver; it is about the heart and intentions. If you are not seeking sexual gratification out of it, you are doing it for the right purposes.

Utilizing Wrap Around services is an effective way to help more clients and get greater traction on their goals and meeting the Golden Thread. Do not forget to take credit for your documentation, have the ROIs in place, and make friends with other social workers. The more resources you know, the better off your clients will be. You should never be a long-term solution for your clients. Your program may be long-term, but you should feel good that you are forwarding to another provider who is capable of helping get results.

I am going to detour quickly. I attended an intake for Case Management for a client who was being referred for Wrap Around services. The Case Manager said, "If you no longer need me, I will not be offended," and affirmed to this client that self-sufficiency is the ultimate goal. At first, you may need to hold your clients' hands, but be careful that you are not working harder than they are, or you are not making them have some buy-in. As a social worker, I had met with an agency supervisor and said, "I'm concerned about the lack of buy-in from the client." I affirmed that if they are not ready to engage effectively, there are others on my caseload who will, and I will move on, hold their referral until they are ready to engage, and then it's my responsibility to not judge them because they came to the party late.

Why Wrap Around services? (1) It helps you do what you cannot or are not willing to do and (2) another professional will help your client with specific needs (housing, mental health, alcohol/

drug, domestic violence) and you expose your clients to many different approaches to solve their case. Maybe your organization has Case Managers and Skills Trainers; the Case Manager is the primary agent and will refer specific life skills coaching to the Skills Trainer so the Case Manager can work with another client while the Skills Trainer is working with that client. Then you find out that client needs therapy. Neither a Case Manager nor a skills trainer is capable of doing this (some Case Managers are QMHPs who are part-time Case Managers), so the QMHP does the therapy and relates back to the Case Manager and Skills Trainer with needs done. Maybe they need psychiatric care; that is where the psychiatrist and psychiatric nurse come into play.

Maybe your clients have legal issues. Remember, we discussed scope of practice. It is not likely you are a lawyer; therefore, the lawyer advocates for your client's legal needs and reports back to you (if there is an ROI). This way, their legal needs and their social worker needs are being met. Maybe they need a housing specialist who understands all the specific housing programs available to them, so refer them to that referral source. Perhaps they need insurance (Medicaid, Medicare, and/or private insurance), so get them in touch with the specific people who are licensed for insurance or approved to apply for government benefits. Can you see how much you have accomplished already for this client all because you utilized Wrap Around services?

In terms of legal issues, unless you actively witness what you are required to report as a Mandatory Reporter, it is not our job as social workers to complicate our clients' lives. I am aware of a client who has an out-of-State warrant. It is my duty to ask if another agency managing their case is aware, yet it is not my duty to call the local authorities (or that out-of-State agency) and tell them where to find this person (as the warrant was narcotics-related bench warrant versus murder, for example). If you as a social worker believe you are a tool of ICE and/or the District Attorney, you are mistaking your mission. Our job is to identify the barriers and how to help clients address those barriers. While a client with warrants will have a difficult time overcoming the barriers associated with an active warrant, there are things that can be done to advocate for them. On that note, drive with clients in such a way that you will not be pulled over because law enforcement may run everyone in the car and your speeding ticket may lead to a client going to jail. For the record, this writer at the time of this writing has never been pulled over with a client.

Let's discuss Mandatory Reporting. I reflect on a weekend where I had engaged with a person who gave me the perception that there was neglect but could not say with reasonable cause. I had discussed this with my supervisor, and it was suggested that the program I was working with purchase some food, and they would reimburse (note, it was not my money). The next day, it was made more official that there was neglect. That next day, I was then required to make a Mandatory Report because I could substantiate just cause for making the report. Yes, that report will complicate that person's and their family's life, yet it also protects my credentials and ethos.

Maybe your client needs spiritual care. Contact the Priest, Pastor, Clergy, Bishop, Cleric, or spiritual leader of *their choice* and let that person meet their spiritual need. You are not responsible for a client's spiritual growth, moral choices, or life choices; you are responsible for your professional ethics and how you have advocated for your clients. If you have documented all your efforts, have the right ROIs in place, and have a good idea who other referral sources are, your clients will be in good hands and the Golden Thread will be achieved. Seriously, Wrap Around services are your clients' ticket to self-sufficiency because every provider will likely have a time they are willing to negotiate the client's needs before the client takes personal ownership.

While working as a Social Services Director for a skilled nursing home, I had come across a client who was a devout Roman Catholic. I am Protestant (proud of this), and I explained to them I am not Catholic but would call the local Parish and see if the local Father could come down and do Communion and time of worship. It was far more rewarding for me to know that I had done what was necessary for this devout Roman Catholic to express their faith. Perhaps you will have clients who are Muslim (it is not your job to identify their sect), so ask them if you can contact the local Mosque and put them in touch with another Muslim Cleric to meet their needs. The challenge may be that your area does not have a Mosque, but it is likely your local colleges will have a student club that can help you connect with Muslin resources. Likely, you will live in areas where Mormons cannot get to the Stake Center or their local Chapel, so ask them if you can contact the local Bishop to meet with them. You do not have to know which Chapel meets their address. Let someone else do that for you. Just make the contact!

In addition, while working at a skilled nursing home, a patient was identified as a Buddhist. My in-laws are Buddhists; therefore, I asked them if they wanted me to share their information so they could "Chant" with other Buddhists. The patient responded, "I am singular in my practice," and I was fine knowing I had done my job to attempt to attend to his spiritual need. Just because I am a Protestant, it does not give me the right to deny access to spiritual guidance for my clients.

I am reminded of a good friend, a fellow social worker. She was laid off and, at the same time, was then hired for a Case Management at another agency and awarded a schedule that included Sundays. This social worker explained she could then help her clients get to church who had no rides. She understood she might not always agree with that persuasion, but helping her clients' spiritual needs be met was of greater value. I would hope, if you are a social worker, working Sundays, even if you are agnostic/atheist or do not prescribe to your clients' beliefs, you would help them access their spiritual health. Sincerely, just because it is not your values does not mean you cannot help someone else achieve them.

When my Father went into the hospital, I alerted the staff that he should not be given spiritual health from a Catholic (or at least not stated the Chaplain is Catholic) because of his belief systems and delusions. I have given them insight into his belief systems, his practice of faith, and how best to meet his spiritual needs. I no longer attend or ascribe to my Father's belief system. That said, it is right of me to affirm his belief systems and ensure that his spiritual needs are being met.

Some of you may be fantastic with resources but do not have the interpersonal skills to work directly with clients but want to see them succeed. That is where being a Services Coordinator may come into play for you. You then manage the referrals, set the dates, communicate back to the lead social worker, and gain the benefit of knowing you had a part of making your clients' lives a beautiful thing. This does not mean all Wrap Around and/or Service Coordinators will not be in the field but rather it gives you another understanding of social services and how we can provide for our clients. Not all social work is with clients. Some of it is on the phone, some of it is on the receiving end of the website request for help, and some is electronic communication. What was just described is more like an Office Assistant/Manager; your scope of practice is more limited, but your impact is immense.

In a previous chapter, the title was worded "Get Over It!" and I want to challenge you to get over your own assumptions, morals, and values. I am not asking you compromise them; rather, do not be abusive to your clients' needs all because it goes against your fundamentals. You are unique in what you believe. Why is it a problem for your clients to be unique in what they need?

Please continue on this journey. Jordan disclosed that (s)he was legally married and working on divorce. There are circumstances that are not allowing for an expedited divorce, and this person reports (s) he is engaged. I purposely call this person Jordan because it could be male or female that defines this story. Jordan sought help with getting some legal documents so (s)he could advocate for themselves. Although I believe in marriage and being loyal to your marriage, it is not my duty to preach to Jordan about their choices. Their morals are not my morals, and as long as they are not hurting anyone, it is none of my business. What you must also know when I first met Jordan is, they had disclosed that they are bisexual as well. Frankly, Jordan might be violating every sacred paradigm in your sincerely held beliefs. That is good. If a client's action help you define yourself, they have done something of value for you.

While helping Jordan, there was another challenge. Jordan had needed my agency to pay their legal document fees; it was less than ten dollars and greater than five dollars. After that was paid, (s)he then asked if I could take them to buy tobacco. Being a social worker nerd, I asked, "What brand do you want?" because I have learned where the best deals are for my clients. It would have been really easy to say, "You needed my agency to pay for your document, but you can afford a pack of tobacco." Yet that would be judgmental and marginalizing. For Jordan, to have a pack of tobacco might have been their sanity break and means of coping with their realities. I want to challenge you. Do not ask your clients in the moment how it was appropriate to need help paying for a document and immediately turn around and purchase tobacco; rather, if later you work with them on budgeting, bring it up and say, "How in the future can we assure you can afford important documents while also being able to purchase tobacco?" That, I promise, will be more effective!

It is completely acceptable to refuse if your client has goals around social interaction and they want to go purchase pornography and/or attend the strip club. In fact, I might add, it is likely in your professional interests not to engage in those types of social interaction while you are on the clock. What you do in your spare time is your business. My local area is small; therefore, if you engage in those activities, expect it to leak out!

Next, I want to shift gears to an incident that offended me and where I felt management then and now lacked heart and compassion and their request violated my conscience. As a skilled nursing home Social Service Director and discharge planner, I was directed by the Administrator to discharge a patient to the streets after being rehabilitated. That Administrator's view was that they came from the streets before going to the hospital; therefore, they can go back to the streets. I have too much human decency to believe that the streets is an acceptable discharge without first attempting another solution. I took upon myself, with an ROI, to contact the mission, and it was agreed to have the client do an intake interview. Problem was, the client had no way there, and I could not drive them due to liabilities. Finally, I got the Administrator to agree to transport the client via the company van to the Mission to determine if they would be accepted. Long story short, the Mission accepted the client, but the client blew out of the Mission. I created an option for that client that did not involve going back to the streets, but they chose the streets in the end. It is never acceptable to me as a social worker to believe that the streets is the answer unless other steps have been done to prevent it. If you believe like that Administrator that the streets is the answer, we need to have a conversation about human decency.

I will later tell a story of the client whom I had discharged to the streets; it was their own choice because they rejected all other efforts attempted on their behalf. If the streets is where you discharge the client because no other suitable option was in reach (in part because of the clients' inabilities to accept reasonable offers of help), document everything you did and why the outcome was justified—the streets.

Recently, I have left my place of worship of over ten years because a prominent member of the church who has preached at that pulpit went public and argued that Warming Shelters are not necessary in my community; this person argued that they promote homelessness and drug use. This is my personal belief. If you are pro-life and believe it is okay to let a born human freeze and not get proper medical care, and/or do not believe housing/shelter is a fundamental human right, I question if you are suited for social work and certainly will not worship where you have (in my words) abused the position of the pulpit.

Essentially, being pro-birth does not make a person compassionate or necessarily appropriate for social work; a social worker must be capable of not using their own biases against the potential success of our clients. You can, as we discussed in the faith community, hate the sin, but that does not mean hate the "sinner." Frankly, I believe (you do not have to) we are saved by Grace, we are born sinners, and none is better than the next. If you share this, I, on a personal level, appreciate you! If you do not have a religious persuasion, that does not disqualify you from social work. In fact, my faith is personal to me, and how I live it is personal. It does guide how I do my job, yet it is not the reason I do my job.

I want to challenge you. Your values, beliefs, and dogma should help shape your ethics but should not be used against your clients (I cannot stress this enough). I am going to discuss in the final chapter how academia and feminism have shaped my training and work as a social worker. I think it could be argued that feminism is a civic religion and my faith is a sacred interpretation of my chosen text and belief system. Not every client wants to know or will accept that I have feminist views. Therefore, audience analysis is necessary. Understand what your clients need from you, provide what they need, and still be honest to yourself, who you are and what you are.

While I was in high school, one of my good friends disclosed that she was a practicing Jehovah's Witness, and that led to conversations about civic engagement and voting. She reported their faith and her practice of faith did not permit voting. As a social worker, you will be asked to assist your clients in registering to vote. It is NEVER acceptable to advise your clients which Party to vote or choose to not identify a political Party; rather, your obligation is to empower them to engage. If you are like my high school friend and your faith does not permit this, it is wrong for you to prevent your clients from engaging because of your faith. Also, Jehovah's Witnesses do not celebrate the Holidays and/or birthdays. It would be unfair for you to not help your clients get help with the Holidays and/or celebrate their birthdays because of your faith. I am not asking you to dismiss your sincerely held beliefs; instead, I am asking you to identify them and help your clients.

This chapter has likely felt like an attack. It is not meant to be like that; it is meant to address issues this writer has seen and identify why it is not acceptable in social work. As you will read in the final chapter, I am a feminist, it has guided me, but I own my beliefs and their reactions (I do not own how you react to this writing but rather how my client will react to how I prescribe these beliefs). How I am in my personal life is not always the same as my professional life. That does not make me two-faced. Instead, it means that I can balance my personal versus public life. If you have never been asked to separate your personal life from your public life, consider this your personal invitation.

Sometimes Tough Love Is the Best Advocacy

If you made it through the last chapter, this may seem like a two-faced chapter, so please read it fully. I worked with a client I will call Jenny, and she was offered every Wrap Around service this writer could think to offer. While taking her to a mental health appointment, I had gone to the Women's Mission and asked the Mission if they in fact were full like the client told me. I learned they were not full and received a full explanation of what it would take for a client to be considered. In the course of meeting with the Mission, Jenny called and said, "I told my Case Manager to fuck off." She said it so loud that the lady at the Mission heard and told me, "Don't even offer her to come here because we will not accept her." First off, I chose not to censor my client's exact words because that is the reality of how this client and maybe others find their circumstances.

I went to pick up Jenny and explained that I had been at the Mission when she called and now she has sabotaged her success with her Case Manager and the Mission will not even consider her because of her mouth. Weeks went by, the client kept crying that she had nowhere to live, that she had to couch surf. I kept reminding her that I had found a shelter out of the county with full Wrap Around services, but Jenny would not accept that. I told Jenny she could not go to the Mission because of her attitude and suggested the Mission one county over. I told Jenny she would not be able to smoke, and that set her off. I explained I do not make the rules of the Mission, and if she wants off the streets, these are her options. It finally reached the point with this client that I looked at her and said, "Tell me where I can drop you off because I am done at this point." I dropped Jenny off at community dinner that night and contacted her primary workers and documented my encounter.

If you have to use tough love, it is important that you talk about this with your manager and document the entire encounter, both via e-mail and your designated EHR. It was the hardest thing for me that night to tell Jenny that the streets was where she was going, but there was no other choice. Jenny chose her path that night by not accepting any reasonable options proposed over multiple encounters. A seasoned social worker understands you cannot work harder than your clients. Jenny, unlike Kim, had no buy-in for her situation, and the failure to have any amount of buy-in made it impossible to change the circumstances. I must disclose, dropping a human off to the streets violated my pro-life beliefs; it was only an understanding that this writer had done everything possible to prevent Jenny from going to the streets that made it remotely acceptable.

What drives me crazy as a social worker is when I schedule a long-period appointment, such as Social Security, and the client is a No-Show or the Client Cancel at the last moment. That is time that could have made two to three other client appointments. If a client continues to abuse the No-Show and/or Client Cancel, you are in your right to close them and terminate their services. This means if they want services, they must return to the start of the line. I cannot tell you how many clients have missed checking their mail, not answering calls, or failed to update their contact information and lost their standing on the HUD waiting list. If you are a Case Manager, please help your clients remain active on these lists while also teaching your clients how to be self-sufficient. I can assure you, HUD does not care what the circumstances are; they will require you to start from the top. If other community partners act this way, feel free to be consistent with your clients as well. I might add, if my agency believes it is prudent to keep a habitual No-Show and/or Client-Cancel client open, they will go to the bottom of my priority, and the burden to engage falls on them. That written, I will make contact about every two weeks, but that does not mean I will attempt to work harder than the client without some indication of buy-in.

I remember a couple who had engagement issues that ruffled my feathers. Previously, they had missed a housing opportunity by not acting on it. Fast-forward, they had requested help with setting up a tour of another housing option. This writer had come back to their area to meet them and got a text thirty minutes before the appointment asking to change the appointment. It was agreed to share the housing owner's phone number. There was no ROI; therefore, I could not tell the landlord who would call them. Instead, I called the landlord to see if the "scheduled appointment" had called them to make different arrangements, and they had. The next day, they had canceled their next critical engagements saying it was a different day when others in the office backed me up that it was that day. It was decided that they would have one hour to text back their confirmation of the next appointment, or the staff would cancel their appointment and move on to the next referral. When a client refuses to have ownership of their situation, other clients can be served. This writer will move on, hold the referral, and if they want to engage, will make an agreement of what that engagement will look like. At that point, the client(s) have asked for "tough love."

I am reminded when I was an undergraduate, I served on the Residence Hall's Student Hearing and Conduct Board, and we had this one student who continued to come to us. In order to even see us, you had to at least have two to three encounters with your Hall Director. We had decided after multiple times coming to our Board that we needed to recommend kicking the student out of the dorms; it was not easy, but it was necessary. If you are giving your clients every chance to change and they refuse, tough love becomes the only available option, but it should be exercised judiciously. If it makes you feel better, our recommendation had to be accepted by the University Executive Team. Just because you make a recommendation for consequences does not mean it will come down to that. The reality is, a professional will do what is necessary, and if it is negative, it should not be a shock to the person receiving the negative consequence.

I came across a client who was kicked out of their Transitional Housing. It was not for violations of drugs and alcohol; rather, Kristy would call her child a "nigger," and the child would call her one back. Kristy had been asked many times to curtail this behavior, and it was affecting the whole house. Therefore, Kristy was kicked out of Transitional Housing. At some point, if a client will not comply with socially acceptable behavior when they are living in a community-based living situation, you must remove them for the good of everyone else. I never want to see anyone homeless; it was Kristy's inability to correct her actions that caused homelessness. A client will sadly bring natural consequences; understand it was their choices, not yours.

As a Navigator, I had the most profound experience that caused me to staff with my coworker and contract payor. The clients were going to close my services, said they had met their goals, but their outcomes were negative. The children were removed, they had been evicted from their housing, yet they closed services "achieved." I was perplexed. How can I say that a client has "achieved" when their outcomes were so negative? Upon discussion, it was determined they had in fact "achieved," but it was self-sabotage that doomed their outcome. It is important in social services to report the facts even when the facts create mystery. The mystery was a negative outcome, yet the clients were "successful" in meeting their goals. These same clients ended up coming back on my caseload sometime later, and we discussed the self-sabotage and how they put themselves in their current position. Moving forward, I told them the past is the past and to start anew. A social worker is in their right to know the past but not let the past cloud their approach to helping them.

I will never forget after getting Legal Guardianship of my Dad, he had abused the phone by calling 911 while his live-in caregiver was there to help him. He was so manic and would not change his behavior; therefore, I walked in the house, disconnected the phones, and removed them. This was okay because he was going to be supervised twenty-four hours a day. Someone would be there to call for help should he need it. When actions require you to exercise tough love, it is best to ensure that you are in accordance with the laws, ethics, and expectations of your employer.

In my years of social services, I have had to reason with my clients, and this applies as a coach. I am a Mandatory Reporter and will do what is necessary to protect the children, themselves, or others from harm. I am not bashful about saying, "I want to continue doing this kind of work," and recognizing that reporting your clients will happen and that it is necessary and prudence is important. If you feel you cannot report your clients, your neighbor, your family, and/or your friends for health and safety issues, social work is not the place for you (including coaching, church ministry, and/or volunteer services). The outcomes associated with the report are not your problem. The clients, neighbors, friends, and/or family brought those consequences on themselves.

Unless you feel it will endanger you or you are prohibited by your company policy, you can communicate to your clients that a report is necessary. At the same time, Mandatory Reporters do have the benefit of being anonymous. Know this, you may have to provide your name to guarantee you are covered as having reported. In Oregon, at the time of this writing, the standard is just cause for making a child welfare report. If you are doing what is morally right, have the facts to back up your belief, and act out of just cause, it becomes necessary to report and let the agency receiving the report to do the investigating.

We discussed earlier about Medicaid/insurance fraud. It is your responsibility as a social worker to report unethical and/or illegal behavior of your colleagues. When I worked at a skilled nursing facility, they had an anonymous Compliance Line established. Congress has passed Whistle Blower Protection laws, and if you want to protect your right to continue in this industry, do what is right both by your clients and our profession. Multiple times in this presentation, I have discussed the idea that we are professionals, and this applies to volunteers, interns, and/or paid social workers. In fact, Sunday School Teachers have an obligation to protect the children in their care, and if you are in children's ministry in your local church, check with your pastoral staff on what your obligations by the church are in addition to being in compliance with your state and local laws.

If you only read this chapter, I want you to stop, start from the beginning, and understand tough love is not the usual part of the social services. Compared to other chapters where I have provided many cases to enhance my point, I have far fewer cases of tough love compared to many cases of compassion and tireless working to help my clients and hope this will be your experience as well. Social workers (I cannot repeat this enough) should not be on a power trip, attempt to marginalize, or complicate our clients' lives; rather, we should be the vessels that may get to places like Richard and Kim ended up getting to in life.

Sometimes, social workers face challenges in their own lives. My youngest child, while we were driving, was reported by another brother that he removed his seat belt. My clients must comply with seat belt laws, and so should my children. If you are not going to be safe in my company or personal car, you lose the right to receive my transportation services. As my child does not seem to listen to Dad, we stopped at the nearest fire station and asked the firefighter to address my child's negative behavior. It is okay to set standards, enforce them, and if that does not work, bring in another authority. If your client and/or child does not respect your authority, find an authority that can get the message through. Being a social worker, you must be creative, impactful, and yes, sometimes you have to exercise tough love. Tough love should be the exception, not the rule (I understand that if you are going into law enforcement, parole/probation, and/or child welfare, this may be used more frequently).

I was once the driver for an old church. It was winter. We had boarded the church van (I was van cleared by the church and their insurance), and I had fellow church members (adults) who were not wearing their seat belts. I told them we were not going any further until everyone was seated and secured. In my exercise of safety expectations, I had missed an important aspect—doing a comprehensive precheck safety review of my vehicle. I had checked my tires and such, but I did not think to check my windshield washer fluid. We hit the mountain passes, and I did not have windshield washer fluid, so my view was obstructed. I want to impress upon you that when you are transporting clients and/or church members, make sure you do a comprehensive vehicle safety check. If your vehicle does not meet this standard, demand from management that it be safe enough to transport. Management may not want to spend the money, so it becomes your duty to impress upon them that human lives are at risk in addition to their reputation. Tough love toward clients may also need to be exercised against management. As a professional, it is our job to do this.

As hard as it may be to not want to help, I will never pay my client's legal fees. That said, your agency may help, yet I will not use my own money. The clients have legal fees because of a reason; it is my job as social worker to help identify why they are in that position and how they can get out of that position. Maybe they need a job, increased income. Perhaps they need help navigating systems that will help reduce their financial burden. Helping your clients navigate and/or identify how they got into this position will empower them. Seriously, your clients may be in jail by unjust circumstances, yet it is not your responsibility to bail them out. I understand that they might lose their jobs; that is a consequence. Before you contact their employer to explain their circumstances, you best have a written and authorized ROI that is specific in scope and purpose (you thought ROI discussions were done?).

If your client needs insurance to keep their license, do not add them to your policy. This goes back to the chapter on boundaries and the fact that you open yourself up to unforeseen financial liabilities. Remember Julie. She had to apply for an SR-22 here in Oregon because she was stopped, cited, and found guilty of driving without insurance. This writer had never dealt with an SR-22. Therefore, I had to nerd and help the client, and she had to come up with the money to gain this policy. And then this writer helped file the record with the DMV. It is totally acceptable to navigate the systems necessary to change their situation, but it is NEVER acceptable to be the personal solution. I hope you understand, the chapters on ROIs and boundaries are not single-minded chapters; rather, these concepts continue to come into other chapters and client experiences through these journeys.

I want to tell a personal story quickly. My own child had been so disrespectful he was warned about his behavior. The ways I was raised are not applicable to parenting today. in fact, many of my clients were raised the same way I was (not saying my parents were wrong), and those methods caused them consequences resulting in my services. I had told my child he would lose this specific electronic device. With continued negative behavior, I took another device, and then he escalated to even more despicable behavior. I, in return, took his TV, all his electronics, his gaming chair, and his branded items that were expensive and meaningful. I explained he would be grounded from them for seven days. If he had additional negative behavior during that seven days, an additional day would be added. Three days in, he asked if he could earn back something. I told him seven days—he has had a change of behavior because he understood as a parent, I was serious and I followed through. I am writing this because when I was working with my Personal Support Worker client, I explained to the client's parent that it was the worst day to have worked with the client, but we attempted to work through why. I shared to the parent what was done to my children, and I articulated my response was due to nonstop inability to listen and get the message and needing to make a strong point. The parent wanted to ground their child from electronics for a week. I suggested maybe start a night, let their child know they want to gain authority in the home, and increase later if necessary.

Tough love should be the last resort as a social worker and/or parent. If all we want is to establish authority or be on power trips, we have lost what leadership, coaching, and social work is about. There is just cause for establishing a standard of decency for certain, yet to jump leaps and bounds into what establishing that authority looks like can either build character in those receiving tough love or make your position of authority considered useless. As a Speech and Debate Coach, I am reminded of circumstances when I had kept a student home from a tournament and also removing a set of students permanently from competing on my team. Neither of these decisions as a parent, PSW, and/or coach are made in a vacuum.

I was invited to a meeting to learn about the benefits associated with clients' insurance and was introduced to a consumer—not my client but a previous client of an employer of mine (not on my caseload). Fred had expressed the consequences associated with not replying on Wrap Around services. That agency had managed everything—if the Case Manager could/did not, another member of the staff did/could. When the client lost these services, other agencies did not coordinate everything, and this client became lost. Tough love is, "Yes, you need services. Perhaps I or my agency can do it. However, it is better to introduce you to a team of professionals that will help you." That would have taught that client how to accept help from other venues and how to become self-sufficient. In this conversation, Fred talked about not having a PCP established and wanting to establish with other services. It was explained as a point of advocacy the importance of doing a yearly well-person check and labs. Fred argued that he would not allow anyone to stick him.

When Fred argued that he would not let anyone stick him or do labs, I had explained that he was going to complicate his ability to have a medical team want to treat him. He agreed to use certain medications—we in the medical profession will honor client choices, yet when those choices are counter to the practice of medicine, they, too, have to respect that it will affect their health-care choices. One must understand, Fred's decision to not accept being stuck and the previous agency setting him up for failure, these are both systemic failures—if Fred had it established that he is affecting his health and solving every life issue will not teach him how to become independent, Fred and the next *Fred* could be better helped. Before this meeting, I believed that my duty as a Navigator and/or Case Manager is to "solve." Instead, my duty really is to identify the problem, follow the prescribed treatment, and empower the client to become responsible for their life (so long as they are capable). I recognize that not every client can be independent, yet the client who cannot become independent is more of an outlier and should be case managed as such.

As my Father's Legal Guardian, I have to advocate that a locked-down unit is the most appropriate place for my Father. It is not my desire to remove my Dad from society; rather, he has acted in ways that make being part of society impossible. As his Legal Guardian, I must (1) advocate for my Father's interests, (2) advocate for a setting that minimizes threat to the public, and (3) become comfortable with acting on his best interests as well. I want to assure that if you are acting in the interest of your clients, family, and/or community, it is void of unnecessary agendas and it is likely prudent.

"It's the Most Miserable Time of the Year…"

There is not a single aspect of social work that does not have trauma and agony expressed because of the Holiday season. It starts in September, in fact. Parents and guardians need to come up with money to buy school clothes, shoes, and then back-to-school supplies. Remember those discussions about Wrap Around services. Your agency cannot be everything to everyone; put your clients in touch with providers who help with shoes and provide vouchers for clothes and back-to-school supplies. The Holiday season starting with going back to school will test your skills as a social worker.

I cannot think of more depressing moments as a child to start the holidays than to know there is "no money for a Halloween costume." You can brighten a life and empower a parent if you help their child(ren) get Halloween costumes. So much of what we do in social services is helping better lives, address barriers to success, and navigate clients to Wrap Around services. Remember when I reported that in all these years of social services, I have never burned out. I am not afraid to navigate the systems more equipped to help my clients. In doing so, I put reasonable limits for myself and get results. By realizing that I do not need to be Super Matthew but instead just a rock star social worker who knows resources and how to access them, I can make a positive difference in my clients' lives and keep myself sane too.

Now next month, in this discussion of the Holiday season, is November. Families are likely short on resources and have likely used all their food stamps before the end of November for Thanksgiving, but having a turkey (unless vegetarian/vegan) and the works is part of the experience. You can do a couple of things: If having a home-cooked meal that is cooked and shared in their home is important, help your clients secure the protein and works. Second, if just having the experience is good enough and they do not want the hassle of cleaning up the mess, I can assure you, every community will have at least one place that will do a hot Thanksgiving meal. Perhaps you have another option—the ability to teach your clients how to cook that meal and your organization approving you teaching them.

In my social worker experiences to date, I have had the pleasure of teaching two different individuals how to make a complete Thanksgiving meal before or after the Holiday. They were afraid of ruining the turkey and getting sick. I remember my Supervisor doing Supervision with me asked, "Did you really spend seven hours with a client teaching them to cook a complete holiday meal?" Remember, my previous coworker had committed insurance fraud concerning billed services not rendered, and he wanted to ensure that I was being accountable for seven hours. He did not tell me that he actually heard all about it because he had inquired the client to verify my notes and find out how it turned out. He was not irritated because those lessons were transferable to any other meal that client in question and the other client would make in the future. Let's review. We have previously discussed your notes. Had my notes contradicted what my manager found out from that client or they were not complete before that Supervision, it would have been a different story. Your documentation is necessary, it is important, and your records can and will be audited. Be ready to defend them!

When I was assisting with the coordination of Transitional Housing, I had gone to my Supervisor and asked if funds would be approved to buy a ham and the fixings to cook the Transitional Housing clients a hot holiday meal the Friday before Christmas. He agreed, also attended to break bread, and the feedback I received as in the future ensured that the clients are a bit more hands-on to ensure that the Treatment Plan is being interpreted correctly. There goes that Golden Thread concept again. I fundamentally believe giving those Transitional Housing clients a proper Holiday meal was a way to validate that everyone deserves joy and peace during the Holidays.

There is nothing more personal to relate to a person than to share a meal that is made with love. Clients will feel it, and you, in return, will feel it. Social work should make your clients feel good, and you, in return, are allowed to feel good about the deeds you have done.

What about children during the holidays? It may be easy for a social worker to feel like they need to purchase a gift for the children, but I caution you, do not do it unless your agency sponsors a child, it is not said *who* in your agency sponsored, etc. Instead of using your own resources and making your clients confused by your act of friendship, connect with Toys for Tots and/or any other social service that is doing toy donations and distribution. You can do a lot of good and not cost yourself money. There is a resource for every need. Nerd and you will find it.

At the skilled nursing, I remember when Santa and Mrs. Claus had come to visit the weekend of Christmas. Older citizens want to experience the joy of Christmas just as much as children. In fact, when the schools come and do caroling for the residents, the spirit of Christmas is lived. The same thing can be said about floats and parades; being in the parade creates a sense of happiness and belonging, and all our clients want to be accepted and valued.

I want to tell a story that breaks my heart because it changed me so much in good ways. My freshman year of college, I was elected Residence Hall President and had contacted the local Salvation Army about adopting a family for Christmas. My dorm raised almost five hundred dollars and donated lots of food. The Friday before we all were to leave for Christmas break, we delivered the food and money. It was so foggy in southern Oregon that we had our heads out of the driver and passenger windows to see because the fog made it where we could not see the end of the hood. We went to next town over and pulled into the driveway of the most beautiful house. We looked at one another and thought we got fooled. We knocked at the door and was transported to the expanded garage. In that garage was the family we had adopted. We made assumptions about them when pulling into the driveway to learn their house had burned down and our dorm made their Holiday a blissful time. It is human nature to make assumptions, and you already know what *assume* means. And yes, to this day, I feel the assumption. Yet that experience taught me not to judge the place and go in with an open mind. Yes, some people are going to take advantage of social services, but the small amount who will are less than those who really need it.

I want to challenge you to help make the Holidays from the start of school through Christmas a magical time. The impact you will have on children, families, and the community will be lifelong. I have alluded at one point to karma. What you as a social worker during this season will create is karma, I promise. Let me confirm. It is okay to enter social services because of wanting to gain warm and fuzzy feelings and because you want to build good karma.

In case you thought the Holidays were done, did you forget about the Easter Bunny? Yes, this is important. If you cannot work during the weekend, notify your clients where the community egg hunts will be (civic and religious), and if you are a member of these civic and/or religious groups, work the egg hunts and brighten the child's experience who only got a few eggs. Some of my best Easter memories (aside from having been the dietary chef that Easter) were the Friday and Saturday before stuffing eggs at church with other members. Hold on, got to explain. My small church stuffed nearly five thousand plastic eggs each year, and it was all hands on deck. Also, remember, when I was a dietary chef, I gave the resident a moment to pull my tail. The simple things in life will brighten your clients' world and give you a lasting memory.

As I write this, I remember when I was younger, my sister and I had made homemade Valentines for the residents of the local retirement home. They loved it, and it brightened their day. Those visits my sister and I had with those clients might have been the only contact outside of the staff they would receive. It is understandable and also shameful in some cases that family will not visit their loved ones, and those visits will be remembered. My points here is, social work is not just about navigating or case management; rather, social services are about meeting a need and doing it with grace. In fact, as a child, making Valentines for the elderly likely planted the seeds of social services.

Especially in mental health and in many respects in geriatrics, the Holiday Seasons is the most miserable time of the year. Clients reflect on the death of loved ones, maybe they are not getting a visit, perhaps their seasonal job has ended as their capacity to support themselves, or they feel worthless because Santa cannot come to their children like he does for the children down the street. I am not asking you to change how you treat your family for the Holidays; instead, I am asking you to realize that most clients will hate the Holiday season. You may need to be extra compassionate during the prescribed Holiday season.

If you are in a capacity to visit a person in the hospital, nursing home, or assisted living; volunteer at a food bank or community meal; or even be part of a choir who sings to the public, those things can change lives, and you will get something from it in return. Not once have I regretted being kind during the Holiday seasonS; I want to be kind the whole year, yet knowing the Holiday SeasonS is not likely your clients' friend will help them. I grew up around mental health and understood that the Holidays are not friendly to the mental health population.

Just when you thought this chapter was about back-to-school and the Holidays, you missed something important—school year breaks. There is first the extended Christmas Holiday break where families are still working yet their children are out of school. These families will need help with childcare and/or getting their children into camps that will allow the parents to continue to work. Then we move to Spring Break; the children may want to do something, the families may want to do things, yet they do not know how to afford it. This is where you can advise them how to budget and save ahead of this (if they likely received a tax return by this point, you can suggest to save some of it for this) or suggest economic activities.

After Spring Break, quickly will come the extended summer break; the children will need either camps, sitters, or ways to remain active. Let me be honest. My community is not affected by gangs as much (it does exist), but you want to see how you can affect these children in ways that being a member of a gang does not become their found reality. Look for scholarships for Summer activities, do an assessment to determine what the interests of the children are, find activities that will suit them, and you will have helped solve problems for your clients. The more ahead of these clients' unspoken needs you are, the most impactful as a social worker you will be.

As we have gone through this journey together and explored this chapter, I hope you are inspired to nerd a bit for the benefit of your clients. Start conversations with them ahead of problems, and should you catch their unspoken problems, you will be able to create answers to their situations. Knowledge is power, but action is empowerment! At this point, the question must be asked, Are you game for this journey? If you can get ahead of the "Most Miserable Time of the Year," your impact on your clients' lives will enhance your résumé, your added value, and yes, you will build good karma.

My experiences with finding childcare for clients have been a frustrating. It is the frustration that leads me to suggest that getting their children in programs that will keep them busy or helping them learn new skills and life adventures, which may in fact change the direction of the children's lives as well, is far easier. Sadly, childcare is not abundant; finding a provider who is willing, in most cases concerning social work, to accept a state-paid voucher is also hard to come across. You will have much more success finding scholarships for camps and adventures. If you are willing to nerd on this subject, the return on nerd time will be amazing.

Be Creative in How You Meet Your Clients' Needs

I want to tell you about "Ruth" and my twice-a-week encounters. "Ruth" was living in managed care, and the Case Manager requested me to work with Ruth to get her out of the house and moving so she would not get bed sores and "rot" without a life of meaning. As I drove to Ruth's residence, I had to go by a golf course and thought, *What about getting the client to play golf?* I asked Ruth if she had ever played golf. She sweetly replied, "No, but it might be fun." And then we went to Goodwill and bought a bag, a driver, a putter, and a wedge. Then we realized she "needed" golfing clothes. In fact, I found a golf course that did not have a stuck-up dress code, but she needed to spend her money to keep from being over-resourced.

That was not the only fun that Ruth and I had together. If the weather was not decent for golfing, we would then go to the billiard's hall and play two rounds of pool. Like golfing, she did not have a pool stick, and she had to ensure she spent her money so as not to be disqualified for being over-resourced. Therefore, we went shopping, found a nice pool stick that was her size and weight, and then bought a case for her pool stick. I want to challenge you. Be creative as a social worker. If you know that your clients need to spend down, why not spend money on things that will matter to them? Remember, I was assigned to work with Ruth twice a week; therefore, the other day, we went to her community garden. During the planting season, we would plant, and that also made it where would purchase plants supporting the clients need to work on money management and budgeting as established in her Treatment Plan.

Working with Ruth, I was able to teach her skills on how not to think about her age and impaired mental health; I was able to help her maintain her benefits by identifying items to spend her money on that were aligned with her payee's approval. Like the golf clubs, clothes, and pool stick and case, we would purchase specific vegetables and berries that she liked to plant in her garden. If we finished in the garden during the summer early enough, we would pick berries that she and her assistance staff could turn into cobblers. The smile on Ruth's face was priceless. The impact of getting her out of the house and teaching her a new skill and hobby were life-changing.

When the weather was nice, during the Summer, Ruth and I would pick berries after going to the community garden so she and her house manager could make cobblers. This helped her skills training moment continue past my clinical encounter with her. If you have figured out, social workers can and should be creative on how we engage with our clients. Had I not proposed golfing, Ruth would never have tried it. One must understand, when we went to pitching, putting, and drive ranges, Ruth did not do *well*, but she sincerely enjoyed it. Ruth and I would rejoice every time she got the ball off the tee into the air in the driving range. The simple things made Ruth's moment. When we played pool, if she hit the ball into the hole, we would rejoice. Sure, I would win by virtue of my skill level in pool most of the games, yet the act of doing something together brought Ruth joy and met the goal of getting her moving and out of the house.

The key to Ruth was my documentation. I had to document what I did to meet her Treatment Plan objectives and how the Golden Thread was accomplished in order for that encounter to be billable. Not all social work will be billable by insurance; you may be a nonprofit that receives grants (those grants are likely tied to fidelity standards), and in that case, the Golden Thread is how your use of the funds to meet your clients' needs meets the objective(s) of the grant(s). See, I warned you from the start, the concepts in this exposé builds on one another. You cannot just have fun as a social worker; you must understand how your work is meeting the goals and expectations while understanding what it takes to be paid for these services.

When I was working as an Activities Director for a foster home, I met with a client who had severe dementia. Sadly, Angela exceeded the license level of that home, and had the provider done her job in assessing the client correctly, that would have been prevented. Instead, the provider was concerned about paying the bills. I am the first to understand the need to pay bills. As an individual with bills and having a Master's in Business Administration, I understand you cannot run a business without revenue. But not all revenue creates a financial return but rather creates a financial liability. However, my job was not to run the business but rather to meet the social needs of the client and create a humane experience for them. As I assessed Angela's activity likes/dislikes, I learned Angela really wanted to have her hair done, but she could no longer handle this ADL. May times, my activity with Angela was simply combing her hair, helping her feel like a dignified lady. If all you do for your clients is make them feel like dignified human beings, you are already doing the greater good.

I have had clients who needed to go on a mental health drive. This is tricky; you cannot bill for a drive, but if you are conversing with the client, finding out what their needs are, scheduling appointments, updating or proposing how their Treatment Plan should be when you get back to the office (or in my case because it was out of my scope of practice to update, I notify the right source what needed to be updated), and reminding them of their coping skills (again scope of practice—at that time, I was a QMHA and not a QMHP; therefore, I would coach them on coping skills trained to me from their QMHP to work with them), then you can bill them. If all you want to do is the sexy work in social work, such as mental health drives, golfing, playing pool, and community gardening, I am afraid you have missed the point of what real social work is about.

I had a coworker who only wanted to do workouts with clients, and that created problems. There is nothing wrong with doing workouts with your clients. Getting in shape, getting your body moving, and getting a fresh perspective is good; however, if you are billing for it, it must be part of the Treatment Plan/Care Plan, or you are not capable of meeting the Golden Thread. Those clients who wanted to work out also received a benefit. I got to work out as well and get healthy. If you are going to preach something to your clients, please be ready to live it yourself! I will never forget "Gene" and our trips to the Table Rocks outside of Medford, Oregon.

My Supervisor reminded me when taking "Gene" out to the Table Rocks to ensure we had fluids and not just water. We would get some electrolyte fluids and hike. We never made it to the top, but we would go for about an hour and take in the fresh air and gain a new perspective. "Gene" gained much benefit from that. Hiking the Table Rocks may not have been explicit in the Treatment Plan, but getting the client to engage in honest reflection, increase interpersonal communication skills, and address issues of hygiene were, and all these are relevant to hiking. Just saying we hiked the Table Rocks was not going to capture the Golden Thread. "Client and this writer hiked the Table Rocks today. We spent about an hour, talked, and in that conversation, client disclosed how his mental health is. This writer listened and suggested ways that he can continue his mental health recovery. We ensured that we kept hydrated and healthy during the experience. On the hike, I reminded the client when he gets home to change out of his clothes, just like reminding him that he needed walking shoes and not sandals to hike the Table Rocks. This writer suggested that he take a warm shower and eat a balanced meal to continue his good health." This is a demonstrated way to meet the expectations of the Treatment Plan and the Golden Thread.

I recognize that I have written about the Golden Thread previously but have yet to demonstrate. I hope the above example of "Gene" and hiking the Table Rocks will enhance your understanding. I want to caution you. Not all this was learned by the end of the probationary period as a social worker; some of it were learned because we have blended multiple social worker experiences, and certainly some of it because of being on an interdisciplinary team experience. If you have read every chapter so far and think you will never be able to do this, the truth is, you will, but it takes time.

In my social work experience, Crystal needed help with getting her lawn mowed, and I had discussed with my Supervisor that I was working with the client on mowing her lawn. It was asked, "How is that part of Crystal's Treatment Plan, and how could you justify billing for your service?" I explained, "If her mental health is being affected by her landlord telling her she needs to have her lawn mowed, by me mowing her lawn, it is addressing her mental health." And because I had asked Crystal to engage in it with me—picking up the apples in the yard, getting the trash around the lawn picked up, and sweeping the lawn trimmings off the sidewalk—my Supervisor agreed that I was prudent and accurate in helping. In other words, your clients may need help with ADLs, basic life skills, or just addressing the external factors of their home that are triggering their mental health. I just want to challenge each of you to be willing to do what is necessary to meet your clients' specific needs.

Frequently, I tell my clients, "We do not need to accomplish the goals all at once." If you are willing to learn, take risks (you will make mistakes; just don't make mistakes that are illegal or unethical) and, most importantly, ask questions. I never met a genuine social worker who kept all their secrets to themselves because they want to teach others how to help their clients succeed. As a Speech and Debate Coach, I do not share with other coaches every strategy I have to win and create a dynamic team—that is my strategic advantage/brand. Yet as a social worker, I want my clients to succeed and the clients of my coworkers to succeed; therefore, I share and write this as well.

I will not forget the day I met with a client (due to the circumstances, I will not attempt to identify this client and/or spouse). He reported he was living in the men's mission and his spouse in the women's mission. I asked him what church he was associated with. He understood why I was asking this, but the problem was, the client identified as Jewish, and the requirements of the mission was to attend the Evangelical Christian church. We, in return, had an open conversation about faith, how I validated his doing the best he could to sustain himself, yet being sorry that he had to violate his Jewish heritage to gain shelter. It was later that day that my coworker reported back to me that the client said that was his first conversation about religion that did not result in an argument. I want to inspire other social workers to embrace topics of religion, mental health, substance abuse, domestic violence, sex trafficking, and LBGTQ because that is where our clients are. You are not being asked to agree with them but rather support them and love them. Compassion and professionalism are what makes you a rock star social worker. Understand how to access resources, and Wrap Around services will come with time and effort.

One of the saddest things I have come across was Julie because her family had let her down. She likely had a Developmental/ Intellectual Disability. At her age, she was not capable of getting it addressed because the age to have it documented had been passed. She was living in a home that was not kept. She had no heat, relied on wood for heat, and had no access to the wood. She needed Social Security, yet she had no clue how to get it. Remember, social workers are ambitious, yet we must exercise caution. It is not against my scope of practice to help Julie apply for Social Security, yet I am not personally qualified. Luckily, in my community, there is an organization that helps people with any kind of disability (in her case, she does have substantiated mental health diagnosis) get their needs met. This can include loaning durable medical equipment or, in Julie's case, help applying for Social Security.

The catch was, they would not transport clients to their office. Therefore, this writer brought Julie to the appointment, watched a Wrap Around provider provide first-class service, and my client was helped. I did not create errors out of ambition, and for the future, I know this resource for the next Julie who comes onto my caseload. Also, Julie had to go to Social Security to request a hearing and get some documentation. This writer transported Julie and then reported back to the Wrap Around provider. An ROI was signed by Julie for both the Wrap Around provider and Social Security. I cannot impress upon fellow social workers enough that ROIs are not a one-chapter conversation; rather, they are the points of access to helping your clients as you can see.

As stated, Julie heats her home via wood, but she was about to run out of it. This writer usually does not work on the weekends;

however, it was validated that this was urgent. The wood benefit was available on a Saturday; therefore, this writer flexed schedule to meet the client's urgent wood need, got Julie the wood benefit that was applied for weeks before, and she maintained a warmer house. If the wood benefit was available during normal working hours, this writer would have attempted, yet it was a Saturday benefit run by volunteers; therefore, the need to adjust my schedule was necessary. The person who helped me deliver the wood benefit (an ROI was made for this individual to know where my client lived) saw that a tarp was needed. As heartless as it might sound, I told him, "You cannot provide everything a client needs, or they will never learn to be self-sufficient." It is okay to accomplish a task, but leave some things undone. Your clients need to learn how to rise above and take some responsibilities for their needs; if you do everything for them, they will be dependent and not mature.

Let me tell you about Michael and Leslie, whom I created activities for as the Activity Director of the adult foster home. I had just married, but I did not have a successful road map of marriage (the last successful first marriages in my family were my Great-Grandparents on both sides). I asked Michael how he and Leslie had been married for over sixty years. Michael was certain in his response: "Just because you are right does not always make you right." That changed my life. In another conversation, Leslie asked, "Dad, how long have we been married?" And Michael responded, "Mom, after these many years, does it really matter?" Immediately, Michael and Leslie began to laugh and shared their love of over sixty years of marriage. You see, Michael was a smoker, but he was not going to quit. He lived well into his nineties at that point. Leslie did not smoke, but she enjoyed sitting on the porch with Michael, and we would all have a cup of coffee and listen to one another. I heard the same stories day in and day out; they both had dementia, yet they were happy and in love. Had I told Michael and Leslie that I had already heard that story, it would shatter them. A good-hearted social worker will do what I am going to teach you next.

Because I had learned Michael and Leslie's stories, I would anticipate what they were going to say and influence the story by being part of it. They never knew why I knew the story, but they sure enjoyed telling me the story for the unknown number of times. If you get tired of hearing the same old stories, avoid dealing with people with dementia and/or in geriatrics. Your attitude will only cause trauma and discontent. Like argued earlier, you are not in the business as a social worker to increase your clients' trauma.

In my work as a Personal Support Worker, I have worked with a juvenile client, Martin, who loved horses. This was the most uncomfortable thing for me; I had been kicked off a horse as a young person and never forgot it. Remember when I discussed earlier the trauma brain? The act of having to do anything horse-related to meet this client's Service Plan brought back traumatic memories. Yet Martin had a love of horses, and it was my job to support Martin in his love of horses. Therefore, I did what I have discussed that was much-needed on my client's behalf. I went to local stores that had bulletin boards searching for anyone who would post anything about horses and would check on social media leads. Then one day, my family and his family were at the same store unknown to each other, and at that store was a horse owner. That lady invited Martin and me out to feed her horse, talk to her horse, and gain therapy.

Remember what I wrote about scope of practice? I was a Certified QMHA; therefore, I cannot provide therapy like a QMHP, yet I can take Martin to gain therapy through his positive interactions with the horse. That met my client's need, kept me in practice, and everyone won. However, horses were not easy to come by; therefore, I checked with my employer, and they agreed that anything livestock-related would meet the Golden Thread if documented correctly. And so we went to the dairy farm and fed cows and had more positive social interaction with the animals. In fact, we would also buy corn (please do not feed the ducks bread as it is bad for them) and go and feed the ducks at the park as part of animal therapy. I want to empower you to get creative with how you meet your client's needs. Martin was a horse man; I hate horses (I go to the rodeo, but that's it). It was my duty to identify my own bias and then figure out how to meet my client's Service Plan.

Aside from Martin, another juvenile client, Max, loved semitrucks. This was up my ally; I was obsessed with trucks as a child and had been a successful freight broker. Max and I would go to the truck stops, get out, walk, and talk to the truckers. You might be amazed how many "hillbilly" truckers are softened when a middle schooler wants to know about their industry. You must understand, Max had some disabilities, yet those truckers told him how his disabilities were not going to limit him. Max had his love of trucks met and learned he can be what he wants to be. I must caution you. If your client cannot be safe in a truck stop setting, you should not take them; if they do not understand stranger danger, this would not be a safe thing to do.

Another juvenile client I have supported as a Personal Support Worker loved watermelon and vacuums. At the same time, Andrew, in his Service Plan, requested his PSWs to introduce him to new foods. Therefore, I would make a fruit salad and include watermelon but also strawberries, blueberries, and maybe whip cream to make fun. As Andrew was also Autistic, this writer had to be ready to experience Andrew's reaction to being requested to eat something other than watermelon. In addition, Andrew was obsessed with vacuums; at the time of first getting Andrew as a client, I had a specialty-brand vacuum. I put on social media that I was looking for a regular vacuum, and a friend wrote me she had one. I picked it up and brought Andrew over to see it. Caution: be ready to be obsessed like your clients. Every week, as part of meeting his Service Plan, we vacuum and clean the house, and Andrew was on a mission to find a new make and model. And this writer being a nerd, I supported this journey to find that new make and model.

There were times that Andrew and I would go shopping for a different experience. We would always end up in the vacuum cleaner and steam mop aisle, and Andrew would tell me what he wanted to upgrade to and what I needed to buy. At an employer, there was a small vacuum in the discard pile, and I was granted permission to bring it home. He now believed that it was his vacuum, and nobody else could use it. Andrew would ask me each week about bringing it home, and I have to remind him that it must stay so he had something to use when he came over.

Andrew and I made plans to tour a vacuum cleaning shop in my local community that also did repairs. Just like the clients brought to the Harley-Davidson store, this met Andrew where he was. As a Personal Support Worker for Martin, Max, and Andrew, I made it a point to do what they wanted and have fun doing it. The difference was, Max was easy because I loved the transportation industry and Andrew was easy because watermelon happened to be the only melon I would eat, while Martin tested my comfort zones and made me relive childhood trauma.

I am reminded of the most miserable/exhausting shift in geriatrics I had ever worked. In my position, I was the Marketing and Admissions Director and had gone to the hospital the previous day to access Ginger and indicated that we could accept her, but there was no established move-in date. My morning had started at 5:00 a.m. when I met Margot and went to the Portland area to transport her husband, Herbert, back to our town where he could get the care he needed. While I arrived in the town to get Herbert, my home's Administrator called and said that Ginger just arrived, and they knew nothing about it. In fact, I knew nothing. I had gone to a business that I had an account with, identified myself, asked them if I could fax our Admission's Agreement to the Administrator to have her start it while I was six-plus hours away.

That night was a trip; the building was torn up because the carpets were being upgraded, power tools were everywhere, and carpet laborers were working. However, before all that madness, I had to help Herbert get home closer to Margot. I had driven Margot's vehicle as I did not want the liability of client transport. She asked me to drive. I did not change her radio station for the exact reasons I wrote that chapter and instead listened to what she wanted and did a lot of active listening. Fast-forward, we had to get the Adult Protective Services for that County involved because the home refused to release Herbert and his original primary care doctor wanted his patient back. The charge Nurse had released Herbert's medications to me. I stopped her. There were narcotics, and I explained I would not accept the narcotics without a valid record of how many started with to have signed off by the Medication Aid at my facility. Remember, cover your ass; that was what I did for sure.

As we drove, an elderly man could only hold his bladder and bowels so long, so we stopped at the rest stop. Before I had left my facility that morning, I remembered to grab disposable gloves and was glad because Herbert needed help with his peri care, and I would have violated universal precautions had I not gloved up. I normally reject the notion of social workers wearing gloves. In this case, I was providing direct care involving possible body fluids coming in contact with me, and it was necessary. I remember Herbert apologizing for the inconvenience. Let me charge you. If you are not willing to transport your client that far and help with peri care, you are not qualified for that job or likely social work as a whole.

When I got back to the home, it was already into the late evening; my staff had two new residents, they had no Care Plans (I was the only person who knew anything about these residents), and the house was in transition of carpet. Therefore, I decided to make it an all-nighter and did not leave the facility until both Ginger and Herbert's Care Plans were fully written. Had I left that night, my NOC shift would have been caring for two new residents without Care Plans or understanding of their ADLs. I also learned something that night. Ginger was a Sun-Downer with her dementia; she wanted to be useful and work. The NOC leader purposely took folded towels out, unfolded them, and allowed Ginger to fold them and feel useful. Being a secure unit, it was safe for Ginger to be up. We were staffed 24/7; my NOC lead did the right thing unfolding folded towels and letting Ginger feel useful. My staff thanked me for not leaving them; it would have been very wrong to have left them. Maybe if Herbert was the only admission, yet having two new admissions in the same day mandated a greater response from me.

In this presentation, I have written about nerding and with just cause. In my County, at the time of this writing, the County Clerk's office is all contained in one area. I had a client that needed a Marriage License record, and we went to one of the Clerk's Offices in their County of residence. It turned out it was not the right building, but that was not the problem. The building we went to also had Parole and Probation, and she thought for certain I was doing something else. It is okay to make innocent mistakes, yet this client was a bit traumatized at first that a social worker was doing something else instead of what we agreed. Had I just nerded a bit, I could have prevented trauma. In terms of resource knowledge, I knew the Clerk's Office was the place; it was the exact location I missed the mark. Seriously, it is okay to make mistakes as a social worker. Be honest and up front that you were in error and maybe what caused the error. If this chapter has not done anything further for you, I hope it will challenge you to plan ahead, nerd, and create benefit for you and your clients' successes.

While at the Clerk's Office, I took the time to ask the secretary if another client had this same need from out of State, would they contact the Vital Records of that State? She said, "Do you have this problem?" And I responded, "No, I am looking to be ahead of it." And yes, I did nerd on my client's time with me, but it was quick, and the next time I need this information, I know the answer: (1) They can go through their State's Vital Records, or (2) if the County is known, they can go directly to the county of record.

I want to challenge you as a social worker, especially when doing mental health skills training, to be extra creative with how you meet your client's needs. I had a client; this person was willing to distracting his mental health in unique ways. I told the lead worker I was going to propose going to the local beauty college and offering this person a professional shampooing and maybe a trim. I was told if that happens, I could work magic. I accepted the challenge. I proposed to my client going and getting a professional hair washing. The experience was so warm and in part because the person doing his hair understood how special that was and recognized that he had some kind of disabilities and made the experience a welcomed experience. We made a point for a while to go weekly for this experience, then he was offered to get his hair trimmed. He had long hair and took pride in its length; the beautician had cut about three inches off, combed, and explained that the rats had been reduced by cutting the split ends.

This client had never been treated to a proper hair treatment. The experience was so positive, and it affected his mental health in positive ways. There was a need to help the client manage his funds, address proper hygiene, and have positive impacts on his mental health. This one encounter captured all these elements and also empowered this writer to understand that social work can be cooking, shopping, budgeting, mental health drives, medication management assistance, getting clients to appointments, identifying community partners and can also be introducing them to some pampering and self-care that will make them feel wonderful and affect their lives.

Everyone Deserves Dignity

I want to remind you, we are all one paycheck away from being in your clients' shoes. In some cases, we are one medical or mental health disaster away from being there as well. I have alluded in a previous chapter about helping a client who has messed their pants get cleaned up and maybe even get a shower. Let me explore this further.

As I was working as a Resident Manager in a foster home, I was awakened in the middle of the night to Steve having a complete blowout all over his bed, on himself, on the floor. It was nasty. I knew that Steve knew it was nasty too; therefore, he did not need me to tell him. I had talked Steve through what we were going to do, how I would get him cleaned up, and that it was not his fault. Understand, Steve could not control of his bodily functions, and that was a reason for needing advanced care. But scope of practice and practicing medicine will be reviewed here. Steve did not have a doctor's order for an antidiarrhea medication, and before 5:00 a.m. in the morning, I had called the on-call doctor and requested permission to give mediation on hand. Steve came to the home with medication but was lacking an order to allow me to administer those medications.

I will never forget that doctor called me everything you can think of and told me never to call an on call during the middle of the night to ask to give an antidiarrhea medication. I snapped back (confidently and professionally), "I am required to have a doctor's order for everything I give your patients. Therefore, a phone order will suffice for now and will fax you a formal request today. Without your order, I am practicing medicine, and I will face that charge." The doctor understood but was still irritated. If you are irritated by OARs and rules of documentation like that doctor, do not go into our profession. That doctor was out of line just like you will be. In the end, Steve had a permanent order to address the situation, dignity was provided to him, and that encounter changed how I looked at helping others.

I had another resident in that home who was a Christian, but his interpretation of sacred text did not allow him to eat pork. Therefore, when I would cook pork for the rest of us, I would ask, "Jerry, what would you like as your protein, and how would you like it cooked?" The rest of the house did not need to be porkless, and he did not need to have any less meal than the others. The same with vegetarians and vegans. As a Speech and Debate Coach, one of my students was vegan. She did not consume any animal products. I had made meals for all my students, and for her, I made a vegetable stir-fry that was fried in plant-based oil and added nonanimal proteins to ensure that she got a well-rounded meal. In addition, I made sure that for Jerry and my student, the utensils I used for everyone else's meals did not get used on their food as a means of respecting their cultural choices. Frankly, it is not important if diet requests are medical, cultural, and/or religious; just respect the uniqueness of your clients.

As I worked in Transitional Housing, Jared required a lot of skills training. He had previously been living on the streets and was rescued from the streets, and I began to notice something—Jared would sleep only on the floor. He had a bed but would not sleep on it because he was so used to the streets. The bed was foreign and not comfortable. We went shopping (a skills training exercise), found a bed he liked, got approval from the payee, and over time, he started to use the bed. It would have been acceptable for Jared to sleep on the floor, but a more dignified thing was providing Jared a bed to sleep in. Just because I have a bed and believe a bed is a healthy way to sleep does not mean all clients will, yet to not offer a client like Jared a chance to have equal sleeping rights as myself or another client is not acceptable as well.

Weekly, Jared and I would go shopping. I would teach him how to get a well-rounded food base, give him confidence to cook some things, and he would ask for cash back. It was his money; therefore, it was not a problem. But I would suggest to him to only take ten dollars out each week instead of twenty dollars because soon he saved enough money to purchase a carton of tobacco a month, saving him money, instead of purchasing a few packs here and there. I want to challenge you. Be creative with your clients, help them budget, and if they smoke, help them save enough to finally purchase a carton of tobacco instead of paying premium prices for a pack here and there.

My most memorable client was McKenzie because she caused me to seek Supervision frequently and even landed me in Supervision. McKenzie needed help with filling her medication minders. Most clients would need this on a weekly basis; I had to meet McKenzie on a daily basis, and then on the weekends, I had to ensure that her mother was given the extra days. During Holidays, I had to be prepared like the weekends. I remember one of the Office Assistants saying, "I think McKenzie really likes you." I am so glad my coworker brought that to my attention. I did my job with a clinical focus, and that made me think about how McKenzie might be acting toward me. It also made me be clear about the boundaries established with my client.

It was late; I had my phone with me after hours. McKenzie had called to say that she "swallowed" something, and I asked her what, but she would not reply. I needed to determine what kind of care she needed dispatched. McKenzie had swallowed tacks because of Pica disorder. I had determined where McKenzie was located and dispatched an ambulance to her location. There were other calls that McKenzie had swallowed a whole bottle of pills not to commit suicide but because of her Pica disorder. Because of my belief that clients gain value by being introduced to animals, we had gone to the animal sanctuary as part of clinical engagement, and I had said something about my Bearded Dragon. Remember, I caution, do not bring your clients to your house. I agreed to let McKenzie see my Bearded Dragon and arranged for my wife to meet us at the park with Ringo, our bearded dragon. I had written my clinical note, and my Supervisor was auditing notes at random and found my note, called me, and said, "You did nothing directly wrong. However, your wife seeing your client even with her approval with wanting to see your Bearded Dragon is a violation of her right to privacy." And it was a boundary violation.

As indicated, I did my documentation of the event with McKenzie; I did not make an attempt to hide I had introduced McKenzie to my Bearded Dragon. I sincerely thought I was doing the right thing; the only reason I was found in Supervision was that my supervisor had done random audits of my all clinician records. The times that Supervision has resulted in corrective action has actually made me a stronger social worker. In other Supervisions, I had brought up the fact that the Office Assistant hinted that McKenzie likes me. My Supervisor asked, "Do you need me to remove McKenzie from your caseload?" I appreciated the choice. Because I knew I could effectively engage with McKenzie—I was not attracted in any way to the client, and I was aware that she exhibited behavior to others to make this claim—I kept my guard high. I so appreciated knowing if ever McKenzie or any other client created issues for me (as a male clinician), I could freely seek help from my supervisor.

Long before I was married, I wore an engagement ring. I have always been proud of my relationship with my wife, our dating, engagement, and now years of marriage. It never made sense to me that a female is given a ring to symbolize an engagement and/or marriage, yet the male does not wear one! My Father worked in the mills; therefore, he, for safety, did not wear a wedding band, and I respect and understand that. For myself, manual labor was not the choice of profession; therefore, why not wear a symbol of my commitment to my now wife?

I will never forget working with Larry and teaching him how to cook. We did enchiladas, homemade clam chowder, and homemade white and red mother sauces, and he learned to cook and take care of himself. He had disclosed one day in talking how he missed being able to ride a motorcycle. Remember my points on nerding? I had contacted the local Harley-Davidson and asked if I could bring my clients for a tour so they could relive in a safe way the days of riding bikes; they agreed. That field trip was amazing. Larry wanted to cry because he got to relive something he never thought he would be able to again. Being creative with your clients' needs is necessary to provide them dignity. It was sometime later I ran into Larry, and he thanked me for the moments we shared and how it affected him. I know not all social workers know how to cook well. I never want to ride a motorcycle, but that did not stop me from helping my clients live in that moment.

Another milestone moment working with Larry was the day his primary worker asked me to contact him. She would not say what the problem was; rather, Larry had an issue he did not feel could be discussed with a female. I called Larry up, and he agreed to meet for coffee. This was a turning point as a clinician; the issue was so personal to him and "embarrassing," as Larry put it, that we agreed to have coffee in the food court of the mall. Normally, having a personal conversation with your clients where everyone in the town can hear is discouraged, but Larry found peace in that moment because the noise would drown out what he would say. Larry needed to talk about his "failed male plumbing" and how "it did not react to his woman" and how "inadequate it made" him feel. Let's review. I am not a therapist, and I am not a Licensed Medical Provider. Rather, I am just a listening male with a caring and listening heart. I remember asking Larry if I could speak to his Psychiatrist about this as it might be medications. "No, she is female, and I do not want to have this conversation with her" was Larry's reply.

My interaction at that moment with Larry could have easily taken me out of my scope of practice. Instead, I just listened and assured him, and when Larry's primary worker asked, "What did Larry want to talk to you about?" I confidently identified, "I am sorry, but it is personal." There was a problem. I had to document my encounter and had to do so in such a way that I could bill for it. His primary caseworker also had access to my notes, just like his Psychiatrist; therefore, I had requested Supervision to discuss how to document my encounter, capture the Golden Thread, and not betray Larry's confidence. In all my social worker encounters, this is the first time and last time I have had to discuss "failures of male plumbing" when the client was not comfortable discussing with anyone else.

On a lighter side of social work, I have been asked to attempt to coordinate fishing groups; although this did not happen, there were clients who would have found value and management and likewise found value in the proposition. The goal was to teach clients a new way to express themselves that did not require getting high or drunk. The agency had secured free fishing licenses for those interested, so they would be legal. Caution: do not agree to take a client who does not have a license to go fishing because then they are out of compliance, and you are you are only helping them create legal trouble.

As I reflect on my journeys as a social worker, I am reminded of a clinician who had an encounter much like mine with Larry. Regis and Donald were the most perplexed gay couple I have ever met. Regis had a persistent and severe mental health illness (SPMI), and Donald was never certain how to respond. Donald, by all accounts, loved and respected Regis, yet there was a day when Regis asked his Case Manager to talk and help mediate a "marriage issue." I remember that Case Manager scheduling the appointment, explaining to Regis that she was not a Counselor but would listen if that was what was being requested. Donald showed up with Regis. In fact, Donald was not certain what benefit would be had. Because both spouses were present, no ROI was necessary. The clinician explained her limitations and made an action agreement between Regis and Donald, and from all accounts, the act of creating that action agreement was all this loving gay couple needed. Again, you might not feel comfortable working with a gay/lesbian "married" couple. I am asking you, set that bias aside and understand they are humans seeking your professional guidance, and if helping them is in your scope of practice, the higher road to take is helping them.

In the chapter "How to Interview for a Social Worker Position," I purposely left this next segment off to discuss here. Anthony was in desperate need to learn how to use the municipal bus system. I had met him at the foster home. On the drive there, I identified the closest bus stop, and before leaving, I stopped by the bus station to gain permission to ride the bus a mentor, displaying by badge and having the client pay. The bus system recorded that I would be riding the bus with my badge, supporting my client. Remember ROIs. I did not have an ROI for Anthony, so I could not tell them who my client was. We spent hours learning the buses he needed to get to school, doctors, work, etc., and that was investing in Anthony becoming self-sufficient. Again, nerding comes into play here; I had not ridden the bus system in years because I lived a county away, so I had to learn the routes, stops, and buses Anthony would need. I am confident my employer would have paid my learning time, but I volunteered my learning time through nerding so I could help other clients on my caseload.

It had been a couple of years since doing bus training with clients. I had Leslie on my caseload, and she needed the bus to get to/from work and her appointments. Upon driving through the area, there were stops that I did not know about; therefore, I told Leslie we can do bus training as part of the social work. This writer needs to learn the new routes as well. I urge clinicians to know where the bus stops by your office are, what buses stop there, and be ready to communicate this. In terms of other stops, connections, be ready to experience this with your clients. Trust me, a few days of bus training will create life-long self-sufficiency for your clients.

In my work in geriatrics, I will never forget Sandy. I was the only male caregiver on the night shift; that meant I was also responsible for the morning shift showers. I had come to Sandy's room and introduced myself. Sandy reported, "Matthew, it took one hundred years before a man had to give me a shower." And I acknowledged what she told me. My approach was to tell her everything that I would do and in what order it would be done. When it came time to address her female parts associated with a shower, I told her, "I will wash you, but when it comes to your 'possibles,' you use the washcloth, and I will help rinse." We laughed that I called her female parts "possibles," but the job got done, and Sandy continued to allow me to help with her showers.

While working at a skilled nursing home, Sam created a case that academically I was aware but never encountered. He was in his eighties but was a geriatric transsexual. He had the top parts removed but biologically was female. Sam identified as a man. He had Medicaid, and that "required" a double room by uniform standards. However, it was not possible to put Sam in a double room because biological men and/or women might be uncomfortable with Sam, and then it was also decided it might be "safe" for Sam to be in anything other than a single room. Management and executives decided that the costs of giving him a single room were acceptable because of dignity and safety concerns. I want to challenge you. Our clients are more than a spreadsheet profit/loss statement; they are humans and desire to be treated like humans. Furthermore, if you cannot accept that transgender people should be treated as dignified humans, you are in the wrong business of helping people.

Remember Kim? I had used my feminist beliefs to try to express to her that she was worth something. Both my academic and Christian training taught me to value humans, not make assumptions of their worth. I wanted Jenny to do better than being dropped off on the streets, yet she made that choice for herself, while Kim decided that getting Wrap Around services was in her complete interest.

Just because you do not have a drug problem does not mean you should marginalize the client who does. If Medicaid will pay for drug and alcohol treatment, help that client get it. You might believe that is a waste of government funds because the addict brought it on themselves. I am not asking you to not believe that; I am asking you to act like a professional and advocate for our clients. Our clients need to know that we are their hero and will do what it takes to get them help. If you want to judge them, demean them, I am confident this is not the field for you.

Let's return to the situation where clients have known legal issues. As social workers, we should help them overcome these barriers. I cannot tell you enough, for ICE and District Attorney, unless you work for them, it is not your responsibility to subject your clients to that process. There is no dignity to that. If they are criminal in a means of hurting themselves or others, yes, report, but ensure that they get the help they need.

As a Speech and Debate Coach, my heart broke coming back home to qualify for Nationals with my team because one of my students, a Junior, told me, "You are the first person to believe in me." She was seventeen going on eighteen soon before she found someone who had believed in her. That same student earlier in the year said, "If it was not for Speech and Debate, I would have dropped out of school." And if as a coach or social service person you wonder if you have an impact, you may very well be the only person to believe in your client and be the reason that they succeed in life. This student was the cause of me returning for a final year of coaching because it was important to continue being a positive influence in their life.

The previous chapter, you were introduced to Julie, and this writer did something that has never been done—took pictures of her living situation. Julie was not aware that I shared the pictures with my agency coworker; my coworker told me that those pictures could not be shared because the client did not authorize them to be taken. The reasons for taking those pictures was to demonstrate how compromised her living situation was and why she needed help. Had I not checked with my coworker, I would have violated her rights in attempt to help her. It is important to do right even when doing right further complicates your client's life. That is part of protecting and defending their dignity.

When I worked in Memory Care as a caregiver, we had two clients who were needing Memory Care and their dignity (and their spouses' dignity) protected. These two consenting adults would be found in each other's beds. They would just take a nap and enjoy each other's company. They did not remember they were married or their spouses living in the community away from them. There was no sexual misconduct; therefore, we decided that we would just observe and ensure that the spouses never heard of it. If there is no harm in the behavior, why try to redirect? These two adults were in Memory Care for a reason. If you are that person's spouse and feel you need a phone call, ask yourself, What would change? I would sincerely take your phone call, yet I would continue to give my resident the dignity they deserve while validating your concern while wondering, *If you did not see it, how did you find out about the behavior?*

If your clients need a service animal, it is worth helping them. Also, be prepared to argue with landlords and maybe prospective employers why these animals are necessary to create value and dignity in their life. Seriously, I understand you might be allergic to animals; therefore, you cannot engage with this client. Be up front with your Program Manager and ask them to reassign this client based on your medical need. That said, if you just do not want to deal with the fur, the smells, etc., I urge you to get over it!

As an animal lover, I understand clients have and want animals, but it is a conversation that must be had—be sensitive. My wife and family for three years were looking for a bigger rental in our city that would allow our animals. We were not about to move without them. However, some clients must move because of circumstances. If they have animals, their chances of finding housing become nearly impossible. As a social worker, especially those of us who address barriers, we need to help our clients understand that their choices to have animals might put them on the streets and/or substandard housing. I am the first to understand these conversations might not be easiest to have, yet it is important.

I will not forget the day that I was at the Housing Authority, and they lamented the clients who will not rehome their pets to gain housing. Yes, as a pet owner, I understand the desire to maintain my pets, yet if I was going to be homeless or live in substandard housing because of pets, I would do what is necessary to gain suitable housing. That said, before a social worker can talk with your clients about giving up their pets, you want to ensure that the conversation is done out of love and respect because those pets are like family to your clients.

In all my years of social work, I have only needed to help one sex offender remain compliant with registration. Jacob had disclosed to me when I helped him discharge out of the crisis respite into a home that he needed to update his status. I was lost. "Status?" I asked. Jacob then explained he had to register as a sex offender, or he would be arrested. His offence was none of my business, but rather, it was my duty to get him in touch with the right source.

I learned any municipal police station can take care of this; it does not need to be the station located in Jacob's city. I promise you, if you are a comprehensive social worker, you will need to be aware of these things. If you do not know what Jacob needs, ask as I did, explain you have never dealt with this, and then make it happen. As I knew Jacob was out of compliance, while we were going to the police station, I will admit, I changed my driving behavior to be perfect so Jacob would not risk being a victim of my pulling over.

If after reading about Jacob you are thinking that this social work stuff is not for you, let's return to Kim. She expressed to me on an appointment shortly after getting her into her place, "Matthew, I had bought some raw meat, a chicken, and put it in the Crock-Pot. I have not bought raw meat in three years." She was overjoyed. At one point, I cautioned you, when your clients get on the train, you best be ready to board with them. Kim boarded the train of success and likely will never look back. Kim's life will never be the same. I cannot guarantee a client will not relapse, but I am confident that Kim has gained so much dignity through the process of working with her that she will succeed. Just when you thought the act of eating a pizza or buying raw meat was a normal act of life, I hope I have challenged you to appreciate these things.

In further conversations with Kim, she said, "It was so much more work being homeless." As a homeless person, she would collect bottles/cans to redeem, make maybe ten dollars the whole day. As a sober person, she is making over ten dollars in one hour of work, has a home, can shop, cook raw meat, and yes, she can eat that pizza too. It is good to teach your clients how to cook, manage their lives, and give them tools for their continued successes. If you get nothing more out of this book, your impact may never be known, but the dignity you show to your clients will change their lives. When I closed Richard, he said, "Had it not been for you, I would not have made it this far." And I am not writing this to beef up myself. I have enough self-confidence. I am writing that to explain your clients need social workers who will impartially believe in them. If your manager throws a case at you and marginalizes what success might look like, challenge yourself to say, "They are humans who deserve dignity." I promise, this will do much.

I will not forget the couple who was looking at buying a trailer. They had me look at the location, and the wife was certain it was the right decision, but the husband had so many negative things to think. Being a business-minded person, understanding social services, I expressed that (1) their current living situation could not continue, and they needed to move; (2) they had an opportunity to own the place, and the cost of buying the trailer was less than seven months of traditional rent minus the monthly space rent; (3) the cost of the space rent, monthly purchase of trailer, and fees were one-fourth of one person's monthly income; (4) if they both work, that means even more income; and (5) their children would have their own space. After a bit, the wife looked at him and said, "Can you please stop being so negative about it and give it a chance?" The benefits of this trailer outweighed the negatives. Sometimes, you must explain things to your clients in ways that will let them see the value added to the decision(s).

One time I wrote a Care Plan, the client said that they were middle-aged and had not gotten their life together. That moment, I stopped writing the Care Plan and explained, "It starts now." I let that person know that they have a chance to write the narrative. I want to empower you to take a moment, show compassion to your clients, and give them hope. Yes, you may have to put some lipstick on that hope. As long as you're realistic and prudent in what you say, that is okay. Clients sometimes need to know that someone believes in them.

I used to believe in part because a lot of my own identity is based on being able to work that everyone who can work should work. As a social worker, I have had this paradigm challenged. For some people, their "work" is getting into A&D treatment, making that treatment, doing their mental health treatment, and once they graduate from treatment, gain the concepts of mental health recovery. At that point, consider the fact that employment is their new goal. I write this because social workers like myself are tasked with getting people housing. Housing requires a voucher, and many are just starting the process of signing up for it. Without a voucher, it requires capital to make the move possible. This is why understanding Transitional Housing, both formal and motels that will write on a weekly basis, is important. If you express to your agency and client that housing is important but paying for it requires capital, your conversation will change and be more effective.

Therefore, I work with clients on finding work that fits their work history, maybe allows their criminal background(s), and most of all, I want to ensure that efforts to get them work do not counter their need to embrace wellness, mental health, and sobriety. If they gain employment but cannot remain sober, the efforts are for naught. If they work shifts that do not allow them to do self-care, rest and sleep to prepare for other obligations, then I have not helped them. At the same time, if a client is capable of working and is working less than full-time, I will express that they need to work on finding additional income, or my efforts are for naught. You cannot determine if work or more work is in your client's interest if you do not properly assess their barriers, needs, and goals. My Father, before going into the hospital, wanted to work. He is on Social Security Disability, has worked hard over the years, and is capable of working. His work ethic made it difficult to persuade he could retire, work on his wellness, and not stress.

In the last paragraph, I wrote about what I respect about my Father—his work ethic. However, my father, in his current state, is very difficult to respect and engage. During a hospitalization, he had sexually assaulted (nonpenetrated) a female nurse and had to remind him of this action. He found nothing wrong with his actions and accused me of trying to claim I was better than he was. Rather, the goal was to remind him of his actions and why those actions were affecting his life now. In a previous chapter, we discussed about Tough Love, yet sometimes, just setting expectations and being creative with how you meet your clients' needs is necessary—in being creative, it may create tough love.

When I started working with Rachel, I had some ideas of her issues from the referral for services. I knew domestic violence was an issue, yet I had no idea how little self-value Rachel had, and my words of empowerment were not dropped lightly. But as practice, she said she "was not used to hearing she's in control," and that affected me. It started this way. She was a smoker. I expressed that if she needed to smoke, she could tell me, and we would stop and smoke. I fundamentally believe if a client is not comfortable when they work with me, they will not succeed—period. When we got in the car, I had my soft rock music on and told her, "It's your car right now. If you want to change the music, so long as it's not offensive or marginalizing with language, feel free to change it." And then she rolled down the window because it got too warm, and I told her, "Again, it's your car. Feel free to roll down the window." She had not been told in a long time that she had control. I do this with any client; however, it meant something with this client because she was used to being told how, when, and what, and to have a male empower her, it changed things for her.

In my years of experience, it also includes caregiving. Manuel was 100 percent disabled, only able to move his head. When talking with him, he said the most important thing he needed in a caregiver was empathy, because in Manuel's mind, if the caregiver did not have empathy, they could not meet his needs. He would apologize about his colostomy bag's smell. Let's go back to the chapter "My Client Smells" and the lessons learned there. The difference is, his smell is not something he can do anything about. He cannot clean himself and cannot control his bladder or bowel functions; therefore, I assured Manuel that he had nothing to apologize about. Yes, it was not pleasant; however, social work and caregiving are not always pleasant. If your idea of caregiver is being a compassionate grocery shopper and cook, you are mistaken, just as much as a social worker who believes it is about teaching money management, applying for jobs, applying for housing, and nothing more complicated.

I previously introduced everyone to Alex. (S)he was a quadriplegic and my first experience. The only thing Alex could do was move his/her head right to left and eyes up and down. No other movements. Alex only asked that his/her caregivers have empathy. In return, I am asking my audiences to recognize the need for empathy and meet the client(s) where they are and do it in the right spirit. Alex had requirements concerning sanitation and systems concerning their care, and if that offends you, I caution you to consider another field.

I want to conclude this chapter by telling another encounter with "Gene". I had heard social workers telling me you have not done social work until your client has fired you. I cannot recall the specific issue; I remember getting the phone call that "Gene" had fired me. That said, "Gene" remained on my caseload. It is easier to "ice" your caseload than to do a fresh intake. In return, I have had to request that a client or two's referral be put on "ice" due to engagement issues that were affecting another engaged client who would have kept the appointment(s) that the "iced" client had missed. It is important to understand, your clients have autonomy, and if they want to fire the social worker, that is their right. It may not be the best choice, yet the act of firing a social worker is their expression of power.

COVID-19

Working Remotely and Still Giving Excellence

This book was in its final stages, and the last thing needing to be done was final edits. Then the remarkable global Coronavirus (COVID-19): hit, and my life as a social worker, parent, and advocate for my parent changed. My Father had spent four months in the psychiatric hospitals; it was clear he was not going to come "home" because of his conditions. We had worked hard between me and the discharge coordinators at his last hospital to find placement that would be approved by the provider and the State. Success, we got Dad placed during the initial stages of COVID-19 having hit America. I was granted one week notice that my Dad would be screened, likely approved, and moved into his "home." That meant I had to pack his stuff, get the legal paperwork in place as his Legal Guardian, and take time off to ensure his move happened smoothly. On a hunch, my wife and I went up a night early to get Dad's belongings moved in and set up like a real homelike environment. That choice was awarded because Dad was not allowed to have visitor the next morning because the State of Oregon had gone into lockdown for this facility, unless it was hospice, their staff, or emergency personnel. I start this chapter this way because COVID-19 has affected the relationship I can have with my Dad. We communicate only via phone right now, and it has affected how I engage with clients.

My primary employer has accepted the changes of COVID-19 to include my position becoming remote from home with very limited face-to-face interaction with clients. There have been some exceptions to the limited face-to-face that the risks associated with seeing clients have been assumed by myself, approved, but not mandated by my employer. What has made working remote as a social worker in terms of helping advocate for my clients, my Father, and my employer understanding the work being done successful is the way I performed my duties before having the consequences of COVID-19. As you have read these chapters, if you apply the principles that have been advocated, have compassion and empathy, and do your work with high ethical standards, working remotely can be successful. I do not believe social work should be 100 percent remote; however, there are justifications for when these restrictions are released to allow remote work with necessary face-to-face, and I will explain them.

If your job is to find housing and employment, question opportunities, or do research on your client's behalf, I believe those things can be done remotely. What cannot be done remotely are ROIs, getting clients to doctor/physician appointments (unless TeleMed is being used), actually seeing the house (unless an online tour is available and acceptable), attending necessary community partner meetings (such as Social Security, Aging and People with Disability, Housing Authority), and getting food bank assistance, for example. As restrictions ease, I see myself doing much more remote work on the above items, scheduling specific appointments with clients to accomplish the above tasks, and then working remotely to document my work and write necessary reports. At the same time, because I use a strength-based case management approach, I have the ability to assess what the client can do and what they cannot do (is this because of barriers and/or physical/mental limitations?) and then help the clients establish a plan to become self-sufficient with my guidance. Personally, as a social worker, I believe the Internet, phone, and ability to conference with clients have changed how social work can be done once the groundwork and sincerity have been established with your clients.

As a social worker who also has a Master's in Business Administration, I tend to look at things from a business lens, apply my health-care background and my case management credentials, and come up with a plan that is medically sound, business savvy, and likely to create results, added benefits, while managing risks. I can see how us community partners, once ROIs are established, can have more online, phone, and distance conferencing about our clients, minimizing our carbon footprints, time on travel, and such, and when necessary, have face-to-face. My hope as a global citizen and social worker is that COVID-19 will have taught us some important lessons that will not be quickly forgotten. I don't want to get political; however, global warming, our human impact on the environment can be partially corrected by how we adjust to the idea of the "new normal" once COVID-19 is in the history books.

I must stress, working remotely complicates things as much as it makes some things easier. Remember ROIs. You know you have it; however, the person on the other line may not have it, or they may not trust that you have it. Therefore, you may have to start a conversation that says, "Can I take a picture on my phone, *secure e-mail properly* [please ensure you do this] you the ROI for your immediate record, and then we can talk?" You want the person to know the terms of what is being released, and that is legitimate. Ethical behavior by social workers is not an option; it is a mandate! Let that person know that once you get into the office, you will send them a formal PDF / fax copy of the ROI for a more official record.

As I write this chapter, I am reminded of subpoenas I have received. Due to COVID-19, one of those Court "appearances" will be via telephone. It is going to be important for my own ethos and my company's credibility that when testifying in court, I be in a quiet place, and when not testifying, I must MUTE my phone (this is good practice on any conference call, by the way) so background noise not associated with my need to testify does not enter the sacredness of the Court. I know this sounds cheesy, but when I am working remotely, I have found it more productive to wear my lanyard with my name badge. I also find it productive to wear jeans. By "getting dressed" for work, even when nobody else will see, it puts my brain in the mode that I am an employee providing a service. If you cannot take yourself seriously, I question, Can others take you seriously? If you want your clients to take themselves seriously and change their circumstances, we as social workers must model this behavior. Clients, like it or not, will model our behavior because they see us as positive figures for their lives.

Working remotely means less face-to-face with my clients; therefore, I communicate clearly with my clients, and I let them and my agency know what I am working on, what has been accomplished, and give them the confidence that although we are not face-to-face, I am there for them. This has a hazard, and my Supervisor asked, "Any problems you are having?" I answered, "I need help understanding how to get my mind to know when my time at the couch doing work is complete and when my time at the couch being off work begins." I am a social worker because I sincerely care about the people I am working with and want them to succeed and want to help them solve their problems, yet I must also manage my own life and practice in my own life what I preach to them.

My clients have needed help getting their Stimulus that was passed by Congress and that they had become illegible. I would normally face-to-face bring a computer and work with them; however, COVID-19 has made it where these are not essential visits. So instead, I can go to the IRS website, and clients can give me their confidential information. I enter it and then log out. I NEVER keep their confidential information that is not necessary for my EHR purposes. I ensure clients write down, respond back to me what they wrote down, and then close the browser to prevent the connection being opened wrongly. COVID-19 has made it where I can see much of this kind of case management being done via distance and face-to-face being reserved for the things that need direct support.

Let me discuss something important. You may not like to wear a mask with your clients, but that is your own personal problem, and it's not responsible if you are sick or exposed to sickness like we are during COVID-19 to engage face-to-face without a mask. As a caregiver, when I am working in the home of clients, I am in their home, and they are not getting out. That is different. However, as social worker, I have no idea where these clients have been, and they do not know where I have been. Therefore, the responsible thing to do is to wear a mask. Personal protective equipment is not just for COVID-19. It is not just gloves, masks, sanitizers, soaps, water, and disposable aprons; rather, it is also Material Data Sheets that tell you how to respond to a chemical spill, a chemical exposure, etc., and you should also include proper foot protection. As a social worker, I love to wear my sandals; however, if working with a client on cleaning their home, moving things, doing a dump run/clean-up of property, sandals would be a safety threat to myself. I would need close-toed shoes with some kind of traction. While I was an undergraduate, I presented a speech in my Undergraduate Communication class, "Safety Is Sexy," and the premise was if you like your looks, your hair style, your skin texture, etc., you do things that protect your sexiness. In social work, we do things to cover our asses and wear protective equipment that protects our bodies. If you cannot handle this, I am not sure you are fit for this line of work!

I must address the next most urgent thing: politics and personal opinions. COVID-19 is a political, social, economic issue all wrapped into one giant problem. If you believe it is a fraud, it is a government attempt to control the people, it is a violation of your rights to assemble, etc. I first want to validate your beliefs, say I totally disagree with you, but that is not my point. It should never have been said to your clients. Even if you take my persuasion that this is real, we do not fully understand it. Good-hearted measures had to be taken by the State Governors and the Federal Government, but none of that matters to my clients either. Instead, what matters is that you are following the rules of your local and state governments, along with the rules and expectations of your employer. Your clients should never hear the political talking point from you; they should only hear what you can do, why you cannot do something, and how you will help them become self-sufficient and resolve their case management needs.

Let me say that last paragraph may have offended some of you. Please understand, you must have thick skin to be a social worker because your clients will offend you; their circumstances, their self-choices/sabotages will offend you. And if you cannot handle that, being a direct provider of social work services is not the right cards for you. If you disagree with me, continue to read because you have found value, and that says a lot about you as well. If you read because you agree with me, I want you to also put these chapters into practice because I fundamentally believe this book, these chapters will change how social work is delivered and how it can become a point of excellence, and your clients and employer will benefit from your dedication. Let me say, if you are self-employed, the insurance company paying you will appreciate you adapting these ideas as well.

Providing excellence during COVID-19 is personal. My Father was hospitalized and removed from his psychiatric care facility in part due to issues created by COVID-19. The facility may think that with COVID-19, the family would not get involved, but when I confronted them on the betrayal of trust, COVID-19 was used as an excuse for my Father's care. Let me be clear. COVID-19 or any other emergency is not grounds for betraying your client's and/or loved one's trust. Social workers, geriatric providers, and others who are placed in positions of trust must live up to the responsibilities associated with this trust, or please remove yourself from these points of trust.

My Personal Journey

Advocating and Parenting Parents

I am no "expert" at this. Why? I am emotionally attached to my family; therefore, I want to caution you that doctors, nurses, and professionals do not treat their family but rather advocate for the families because we are looking at a distorted lens! That is why this chapter is called *advocating and parenting* instead of treating. It is okay to review your loved one's Care Plan/Treatment Plan to ensure that it is capturing what is necessary, but you cannot succeed if you are the one acting on it. My maternal Grandmother took care of my Great-Grandmother for years before she died. I moved her in, took care of her, advocated for her, and she said it was a mistake. She loved her Mom and did what she thought was best, but best would have been yes, move Great-Grandma in, but do not be solely responsible for her care. Remember the chapter "Self-Care"? Yes, even with family, you need self-care. Let them live with you, but ask others to carry some of the burden. It is okay to validate to yourself and your loved ones' needs to request help and/or respite care.

My Father is aging rapidly, his health and mental health failing. I will never forget Christmas Eve my Freshman year of college. I had come home, and my late Grandpa said it was my turn. My Father needed to be placed into the local psychiatric unit/hospital. Fast-forward several years, I had to get Power of Attorney for my Father. Fast-forward few more years, I moved my Father two miles from my house to better care for him and advocate for him. And then fast-forward again, I had to get Legal Guardianship because he was in the psychiatric hospital unable to manage *his affairs.* I write all this because ROIs, scope of practice, compassion, knowledge of resources, and self-care are all parts of me being able to successfully advocate and parent my aging Father. I *do not believe* children and family can care for and advocate for a loved one if any of the above are missing!

When I first became my Dad's advocate, I knew nothing professionally. I knew where the psychiatric hospital was geographically located but did not know where in the hospital to find it. I had to ask, "Where is the psychiatric hospital?" And oh my, it was an alumnus from that June's high school graduation I had to ask. We discussed earlier about stigma, and to this day, I remember telling myself, "I just asked my high school classmate where the psychiatric unit is located. It is not like I was asking where's the cardiac unit." To this day, I wonder if she sees me, would she remember all these years later that I had asked her where the psychiatric unit is located? Stigma not only affects our clients and family members but also affects those advocating.

As my paternal Grandma aged, I became her advocate as well. She, too, was mentally ill, and I would never forget the phone call that changed everything. "I thought it was heart disease that would take me out, not cancer," reported Grandma. I fundamentally believed the day she was diagnosed with cancer was the day she died; her death certificate to prove it was delayed. In fact, Grandma argued, "Unless you have had a mental health disability, you have not lived." She honestly thought it was the greatest gift on earth. You have to understand, Grandma and my father lived with each other after my parents' divorce, and she helped balance Dad. When she died, my Father became responsible for himself. All his life, he was looked after by both parents, then he married, divorced, and moved in with Mom again. Then his Father triaged what he could before I actively intervened by moving my father down closer to me.

All my experiences in formal social work were guided by how I had advocated for Grandma and my Father. As my Grandma was dying in the hospital, I would never forget the insensitive doctor;

he had no compassion or warm feelings. The RN of my Grandma's primary doctor had called me, "If that was my husband in your Grandma's situation, I would call an ambulance and move him to the next hospital." That doctor called me, ripped that RN for being what he called unprofessional for talking to me like that (I agreed with her), and said, "Besides, I have credentials at both hospitals," to make it worse. When I write through this exposé about being professional, about your ethos, it is not because I want to sound big and mighty; it is because of doctors like this who have shaped my social service paradigms. If you feel like you have power and that you can abuse that power like the referenced doctor, please do not become one of my community partners and/or coworkers because I would rather work with that RN instead!

My late Grandpa, before moving my father closer to me, wrote out a checklist for Dad to follow on his medications, attempted to help him shop for groceries that created balanced meals, and developed a plan to address domestics. Nonetheless, Dad was not capable of surviving on his own; he was merely living moment to moment. During one of those "moments," Dad had found himself back in that same psychiatric hospital I had checked him in that Christmas Eve years before. This time, the hospital called and said, "According to the rules of Medicare, I can no longer keep your Father, but he should not be going home alone. What is your plan?" I assured the doctor that in thirty days, I would move my Father down closer where I could help manage his affairs, and in thirty days, that did happen, but it was nearly impossible.

Grandma had owned her trailer outright, and in her will, it was granted to Dad, yet the space was rented. For thirty days, I attempted to sell Dad's trailer for below market value under the circumstances, and on the last day, I had made an agreement with the trailer park manager to sign the trailer over to them free and clear at a loss but a net benefit to my Father, relieving any responsibility of paying space rent until new owners could be found. Understand, the trailer park manager did not have to do this; my Father's estate legally could have been required to continue paying space rent until new owners bought and/or moved the trailer. It was compassion on the trailer park manager's part knowing how bad my Father was that allowed this. Had my Father also died like Grandma, naming myself as the Estate Executive, I would have legally been responsible for paying that rent until sold or the trailer removed from the property. It is due to this fact that I will never own a trailer in a park because medical and death circumstances should never affect the owner's children and/or Estate Executives. If you are reading this and never knew it, be prepared for this shock (remember, this is in Oregon, and maybe things have changed, but that was my experience and was valid at that time).

When my Father needed Medicaid, I had to justify why I gave his trailer (a resource of value) away. I have seen patients at the skilled nursing home needing Medicaid and quailing for Medicaid, but because they had given resources away in the last five years (that is Oregon standards at the time of this writing), they had become disqualified for a period for Medicaid. As I could justify why the trailer was signed over, it did not disqualify my Father. But had I signed the trailer to any other party than the trailer park, it would have likely been a disqualified transaction. If you think that you will not be in the five-year window of problems, life happens quick. Most of the patients who came into the skilled nursing home did not plan to have previously been in the hospital and then the nursing home. Life happens on a moment's notice, and we as social workers and advocates need to be prepared to act and assess the barriers to our clients' successes.

It is sad, but a geriatric person with mental health issues in Oregon struggles to get the support they need without Medicaid. Time had passed, and my Father had become eligible for Medicaid. That allowed Dad to receive formal Case Management, therapist, and psychiatrist. Previous to Dad qualifying for Medicaid dual coverage, my Father and my grandma had a very good insurance broker; he had written Dad a supplemental policy for Medicare that covered 100 percent of hospitalizations. It was not cheap, yet the amount spent in one year was less than the 20 percent Medicare did not cover for my Dad's weeks-long psychiatric hospitalizations. Let me caution you. If you do not think you can afford a supplemental insurance policy, just have a hospital stay followed by a skilled nursing home stay; the clients I negotiated with while in the nursing home as a Social Service Director and my Father either benefited or were in tears because of their financial situations. During Open Enrollment for Medicare next time, sign up and/or renew your supplemental policies because you cannot afford not to.

My Father having dual coverage—Medicare as primary, supplemental as secondary, with Medicaid as a third payor—has affected him in so many positive ways. It is a crime in my opinion that people who are private pay and/or Medicare only get less options available to them. My Father and others get transportation paid for medical appointments because of Medicaid, while patients I saw at the skilled nursing home had to pay one hundred dollars to be transported to weekly appointments and/or discharge appointments. If you are a legislature and/or legislative advocate and can pick up this issue, many patients in skilled nursing, foster homes, assisted livings, and/or living on their own (or with family) will thank you!

Like my journey being a social worker, I never wanted to be asked to be my Dad's Legal Guardian. In fact, I fought the notion because I know the responsibilities and implications of guardianship. But I am my Dad's Legal Guardian because of my belief that my Dad needed an advocate who could speak for him and help find placement that was best for him, so I accepted the role of Legal Guardian. Being a social worker for payment is not much different than being my Dad's advocate. Scope of practice still applies, ROIs are necessary to understand, self-care is urgent, and there's an understanding that it is not ethical for me to practice social work on my Dad because I am emotionally involved, but I can use my understanding to get results.

Because I have worked in all but one aspect of geriatrics, I have applied that training to become a social worker and advocate for my Father. The one area I have yet to work is home health, but as a discharge planner for the skilled nursing facility, I made referrals to several different agencies of patient choices and used my understanding of those different agencies to determine which was best when Dad needed this service. My Father needed a foster home when I moved him down to southern Oregon nearer to me, but as a private-pay citizen, he could not afford that. My wife's Aunt had an opening at her spare room, and she was trained in mental health and aging. Therefore, at the end of my Dad's final thirty days living and attempting to survive on his own, I moved in with my wife's Aunt, and he stayed until now when Legal Guardianship was granted. To clarify, it was not getting Legal Guardianship that caused Dad's living situation to change; his care needs exceed his ability to live responsibly in the community.

It's important for social workers and families to understand the levels of care. There are three different levels of foster homes licensed in the State of Oregon. My Father, when he first moved down closer to me, would have qualified for Level 1, yet his current situation would necessitate a Level 2 so he can age in place. At some point, he might make it into a Level 3 foster home where he will gain the advanced nursing skills in a homelike environment. At this point, Dad requires a secure unit placement.

There are multiple types of secure unit placements, and not all of them accept equally. The secure units are the Residential Care Facilities (if a client knows the code, they can check themselves in/out) (with Legal Guardianship, that changes things), Memory Care facilities (they must have a memory care diagnosis for these specialty/licensed facilities), and Enhanced Care Facilities (I am aware of them but have never been in one yet to tell you about them). It is important that you do not place your loved ones in any of these facilities if you do not understand the licensing level and their ability to age in place and if you have not read the State inspection, or that is not going to meet their care needs. Just because you must find something does not mean that you just pick something; this is an important decision, and a qualified social worker should help you through the process. That qualified social worker can be in the form of a discharge planner, a State worker, and/or a Marketing/Admissions Director for the property you are looking at. If the Marketing/Admissions Director is ethical, they will not accept your loved one unless it is right for the facility as well. Accepting and/or admitting someone just to pay the bills of the facility is wrong and harmful.

It is possible that you will do what is best for the moment and need to reevaluate that decision later. For the moment, I had to move my Dad within thirty days; that decision lasted living with my wife's Aunt for nearly eight years. The reality is, that could have only lasted for months and would have still been the right decision. Dad could not live and/or survive on his own and needed to be where I could help manage and advocate for his care, and the gamble was to move in with my wife's Aunt and then plan for the future.

In planning for the future, my Dad's Medicaid Case Manager gave some homework/mandate that I will forever be grateful: requiring that my Dad's funeral expenses be paid for ahead of his death. Dad is a Pentecostal, and his interpretation of Dad before his death, even up to his death believed the Pentecostal faith is that cremation is not right because his body cannot rise and be made more perfect unless buried. The funeral director found a cemetery for us to contact that was economical. Let me tell you a story. I picked Dad up one weekend afternoon and met with the caretaker of the cemetery, and he showed us the available plots. I asked Dad, "Where do you want to spend eternity?" (I believe and know my Dad will be in Heaven, so it was a matter of where he wanted his plot to be.) Dad picked the exact spot where he wanted to be buried. We made up a bill of sale, purchased it, and the deed was mailed shortly after. Now that my Dad is removed from this earth myself and the family no longer had to worry about his final medical care needs or having to pay his funeral expenses and/or purchasing his plot. Rather, we were able to plan a beautiful Celebration of Life that was representative of his faith and humanity. This was a gift. If you do not want to think about death because it is scary and gory, do you really want to plan and pay for all of it at once?

If you cannot tell, I am a born-again Christian, so is my Father (and Mother), yet we disagree on persuasions of the Christian faith. When my Father was in the hospital, resulting in myself gaining Temporary Guardianship, I did not call my Pastor. Rather, I called my Dad's Pastor to seek guidance. I wanted to honor my Father's faith by seeking guidance from someone who understood my Father while respecting my heart and differences. If you are not of faith and your loved one is of faith, you owe it to them to honor their faith. I could have saved money by believing that when my Father dies, he could be cremated and not know the difference. But purchasing a plot honors my Father in death, and seeking spiritual counsel from his faith honors his faith. Those things will create good karma. No, I did not do any of this for karma's sake, but when karma is not respected, the results will not be your friend!

My Father is both mentally ill and has failing kidneys and is likely battling dementia. Because of my work in geriatrics, I know something about this. Kidney dialysis requires adherence to dialysis schedules, diet/fluid restrictions, and travel restrictions. My Father will not accept the restrictions on fluid and diet; therefore, I will not allow him to go with dialysis (as his Legal Guardian). But I did something else. When my Father was diagnosed with kidney failure, I talked to him about his choices and the consequences of his choices, and he asked me not to go with dialysis. Therefore, I know my Father's wishes and also know what is best for him. It is from both of these that I reject doing dialysis for my Dad.

I could have avoided the need for Legal Guardianship today had I forced the conversation earlier with my Dad—Advanced Directive. My Father did not have POLST and/or Advanced Directive because we did not expect him to decline this quick. In fact, reality is, he could have been in an accident and immediately been in this state, and a POLST and Advanced Directive would have been beneficial. Therefore, I am pleading with you, your aging loved one, and/or those with disabilities to have POLST and Advanced Directives while they legally can sign them. My Father legally cannot sign an Advanced Directive because he is not legally capable of making his own decisions. Yes, I had POA, but it was not for his health-care needs. Therefore, I had to get Legal Guardianship to ensure that I could advocate and get my Father the advanced psychiatric care and final placement he needs. If you take nothing else from this chapter, do not wait. Act and talk with your loved ones. If you delay, you may also be their Legal Guardians when lesser would have been okay.

Let me revisit the last paragraph. Because of where my Father had been placed in a facility, Legal Guardianship had become necessary; however, I could have advocated for his acute hospital care without Legal Guardianship had I been proactive and gained Health Care Power of Attorney a long time ago. Guardianship is now necessary; however, it could have been done over time instead of immediate had the first steps been taken. We all understand, preventative measures are always better, in my Dad's case, having had the necessary documents and legal orders in place could have helped me properly advocate for my Father and will help readers if they, too, are proactive before an emergency escalates what becomes necessary. I hope I have inspired someone to understand, first things first are needed first thing before an emergency escalates what becomes necessary.

As my Father was previously discharged from the psychiatric facility in the hospital, it was his longest stay to date and also his first stay since having gained my mental health credentials and extensive experience. As discussed earlier about scope of practice, I ensured the doctors and treatment team managing my Father's acute stay understood that I was not going to practice medicine or dictate (even with Legal Guardianship) what was necessary. Rather, I asked them to understand that nearly twenty years of understanding is known by me concerning my Father. With my Father, I had much more flexibility with boundaries and scope of practice issues than with a client who is assigned by my work. I used all my understanding of his medical history and advocated for what seemed best for my Dad. I want to challenge you. Do not think because you have training that you cannot use it; do not think because you have training that you can dictate what is best. We should advocate and navigate the systems necessary for our loved one's success.

I have had to identify to the social workers, the insurance company, and any Wrap Around provider for my Father that I have QMHA-level credentials, am skilled in geriatrics, and have twenty years of understanding of my Father's health, yet that does not qualify me to care for my dad. Rather, it qualifies me to properly advocate. As my Dad's Legal Guardian, the most restrictive thing I have done is limit his use of telephone because he would make calls all night long and not get well by being hypermanic on the phone. My confidence in my understanding of the complex mental health systems, geriatrics, and my Father's persuasions of faith and wishes do not qualify me to anything more than advocate and contribute through rigorous discussions what might be best for my Dad.

I remember Dad started out with full resuscitation, and three months later, the doctor suggested it was prudent to change my Dad to Do Not Resuscitate (DNR) because he would never have quality of life if brought back to life upon an emergency. I told the doctor, "You are the doctor. I am the Legal Guardian who has to approve. However, I trust your medical degree and judgment." So I authorized the new DNR change. It is not easy, but it is vital to let the health-care professionals do the job they are trained to do.

Earlier I spoke about having paid for my Father's burial and funeral needs. Everything I did was an act of honor for my Father. Paying for it was fulfilling the wish of Senior Services to ensure that this was done. In honoring my Father, I went with a funeral home that had a Christian paradigm because if he is going to die one day, why not support a business that has a faith component to it? I believe our actions must be dignity-based. If you work for a secular company/agency and are tasked with finding a funeral provider for a client and/or family, you may have to operate under a business model of least expense. Either case, you are doing what is right. In my case, it was proper to fund a business that had some similar belief system.

As I brought my Dad out of his longest psychiatric setting, I had informed him that things were going to change. He could not be allowed to roam freely; he needed to have no access to a phone during sleeping hours and needed to adjust back to the community as it was so long being in the hospital. Being nearly forty, my Father did not appreciate his junior telling him what to do or how life was going to be, yet in order to enforce that things were changing, he had to understand the rules. If you are seeking Legal Guardianship to be a taskmaster, please avoid it; that is not a successful Legal Guardianship and/or social service model. We should be compassionate advocates. Everything that we do should be for the greater good. Our clients and/or family may disagree with what the greater good is, but if your intentions are just, your actions will likely follow. Just like I did with talking with my Father's clergy, check your actions against another person. The more people who can speak to your potential defense, the better protected you are. Remember, covering your ass is not just for social workers but also for family helping families.

For myself, I do not want to be buried; I better be cremated. In fact, I better be donated to science, and my organs, if capable, be donated to serve another life and cause. It is important that I communicate that to my loved one who will manage my final demise on Earth. Why do I write this? Maybe the Holidays are approaching when you are reading this, so engage in these difficult conversations. Like written earlier, Dad and I talked about his failing kidneys immediately upon diagnosis instead of me having to make independent decisions. Your loved one will trust you to act on their behalf, but maybe they had specific wishes, and without you asking, you would not know. It does not apply to my case, but maybe "No Blood" is their mandate, and if you do not ask or provide them blood in error, you may fracture your credibility and relationship. Because I spoke openly with my Dad, I learned he demands to be buried instead of cremated. I arranged for his funeral expenses, which are now paid for and the plot purchased. We are now just waiting for Jesus to call Dad to his Home, and I rest knowing I have honored his wishes. I fundamentally believe that in this chapter, this paragraph is the most important takeaway.

I hope as you can tell, my journey to becoming a social worker really started on the day I put my Dad that Christmas Eve in the psychiatric hospital. Looking back nearly twenty years ago, I would not have believed I would be where I am today. Take risks, act judiciously, and if you are compassionate, you will go far. If you have learned anything about my journey taking care of my Father, I hope you will learn something as I delve into my academic and introduction to feminism journey. If you are offended by what I wrote, that is okay; as humans, we do not all see eye to eye. Rather, the point is to learn something and empower the willing to become a social worker or become a better social worker/advocate.

One must understand, my Father has resentment and hates that his child is his Legal Guardian or has any authority over his life. He did not contest it legally; however, he expresses it. Just as I tell my clients when they are in my car and/or office to feel free to express themselves, it is important that we as providers for our parents allow them to vent. If we as providers for our parents treat them any different than our clients, we are doing a disservice. For my parents, I am willing to test boundaries that I will not do for clients, but that is the only difference.

No amount of formal education taught me how to advocate for my Father. Getting original Power of Attorney, acquiring Temporary Legal Guardianship that resulted in Permanent Guardianship, those were learned by my work in geriatrics and gaining my license as a Senior and Adult Foster Home Resident Manager. My education taught me how to research, how to run a business, and how to communicate. If you think you need a degree to accomplish this, you are selling yourself short. An education refined transferable skills I already had. No amount of education will teach you compassion. As I gained an awareness of feminism, my education introduced me to new ways to consider compassion, but I was already compassionate as a starting trait. It is also my desire to campaign to remove the stigmas associated with accessing and continuing mental health treatment that drive me in my own mental health journey, my late Grandma's, and now Father's mental health journey.

I want to conclude this chapter with a word of caution to advanced social workers. There was a hospital social worker who called me and said, "As your Dad's Guardian, his placement is your responsibility." And seriously, that is not true. It is my duty to authorize, cooperate, give input, yet it is the social worker/discharge planner's job to find the right placement. It is their job in Dad's case to get it approved by Senior Services, and then it is my job to support the process. Do not become so full of yourself that you act like this uncompassionate social worker and become offensive and ineffective. If you are dealing with this kind of worker, do not hesitate, like myself, to reach out to the powers that can advocate for yourself and your loved one. Not all social workers are kind and compassionate; some got their social worker credentials through education and their internship without having really worked at the junior level before advancing into advanced clinical social work.

I leave you with the words of the sacred text, "What you have done to the least of these, you have done to me." And that is how I lived the advocacy of my late Grandma, my now deceased Father who was alive up to the date and phone call that this book was accepted for publication.

My Personal Journey

Academic Foundations
and Feminism

I started this journey's story by announcing my going into social services as an accident. Also, going to college was an accident. Had it not been for moving in with my paternal Grandparents, I do not believe college or an advanced education would have happened. I was homeschooled and, to this day, believe it was not a point of success, and my Grandparents enrolled me in public school. Not only that, they also put Coach Michael DeRobertis in my life, who, with his strong words, changed my life. I have always had a heart for people; never did I know it would be my means of supporting myself, and I have no regrets.

My faith has driven my life. As a Protestant who has explored different faiths and belief systems, I have come to terms with my God and expression of faith. I do not feel it is my job to persuade you to accept what I believe. If you are not a feminist, that is okay; it not a requirement to be a social worker any more than an advanced education. Yet I must acknowledge, feminism, advanced education, and my faith guided me in how I perform my job. I want to see everyone come to know my Lord and Savior, see them in Heaven, but at the same time, I want to validate the person who rejects these notions and show them that I respect, value, and love them equally. In fact, the act of love and compassion, as I have argued through this book, is what makes a person a good social worker.

I grew up believing that feminism was about bra-burning and hating men. It was not until I became a feminist scholar that I really understood it is about understanding; acknowledging privilege, power, and biases; and wanting to bring another person forward with me. I will never forget the day I was sitting in Dr. Alena Ruggerio's class and read works by bell hooks (the lowercase name is not a typo); hooks' writings helped me understand that everyone can be a feminist and that if we are all on board with addressing toxic masculinity, oppression, and dominance, it does not matter if you are male, female, nonbinary but rather all united for a better society. As I began to enter my final year of my undergraduate, I realized I was only two courses from earning my Women's Studies minor, and in many respects, my minor has influenced my professional journey more than my major courses of studies.

During my Women's Studies scholarship, I was introduced to Peggy McIntosh's piece "White Privilege: Unpacking the Invisible Knapsack." And as a born white male, I never thought much about what it meant and that my biology and skin color granted me special status. I am not asking anyone to give up their status; rather, I am asking you to be aware of your status. If you have a house or even a secure place to live, you may have more than your clients. Maybe you do not have to take public transportation to every place, so count your blessing. Were you capable of eating three meals and get your fill for the day? I have come in touch with clients who had gone days without a proper meal, who had housing where their landlord was taking their rent money but not providing a safe place, or who could not go to work on a Holiday or weekend because the bus was not running. Like my book title, there are likely other people you know who would give anything to have a pizza without question or desire to cry that there are no bad days.

As a Women's Studies scholar, I was taught to appreciate the Reverend Dr. Martin Luther King and his writings. To this day, I hope my children's character will be decided not by the color of their mother but rather the content of their character. My prayer in social services is that I have valued the person, not marginalized them, that I have defended the uniqueness of the human experience, and that I am open to learning from my clients. As you can tell through this journey, I am a bit liberal (not the political definition of this word) with my definition of social services. If you are meeting a person's need that they cannot meet, that is social services. Therefore, coaches, clerics, pastors, professors, geriatric providers, and support staff and those you have come to understand as social workers are all in the business of human services. How we do our jobs or how we document, bill, volunteer, get paid, or just act out of good hearts is the difference.

I am honored to report I married into a gay, biracial family. My wife is not Caucasian, and diversity makes the world go around. My in-laws are also Buddhists and myself Christian, and we have made a point from day 1 not to let the differences in our lives separate us. By being open and learning that diversity is the key to success (if you are going to go into social work especially), I have become a better person.

As an undergraduate, I had volunteered doing weekly meals for the homeless or food insecure and then also became an organizer and volunteer with Northwest Seasonal Workers Association. My proudest moment as an organizer was being called a "Communist" because I was asking others in my community to donate food to our cause. If believing that you cannot be pro-life and let people starve makes me a Communist, keep calling me so. I consider myself fairly conservative, liberal on some social issues, because my belief system should not be forced on the masses, yet as indicated, I do not press those conservative values and beliefs on the masses any more than I press my faith and interpretation of faith. My public execution of my job is maybe appearing more liberal. People are unique; Matthew is unique. Why would I want everyone to act and conform to my ideals?

One of the most important aspects to my career in social services is the fact that not one academic class was meant to make me a social worker. I took Women's Studies—approved curriculum; however, I did not believe or know years after graduating that I would become a caregiver, a Certified QMHA, a Resource Navigator, and/or a strength-based Case Manager / Skills Trainer. My compassion and passion for humans and addressing poverty, injustices, and believing in equal opportunity has driven me. The last successful first marriages in my family were my Great-Grandparents on either side; therefore, what right does anyone who has affected me have to say who can marry and what makes marriage sacred? If that offends you, I challenge you, invest in your marriage and then let's talk. At the time of writing this, my wife and I have nearly made it further than my parents' marriage, and we have so many more to go together.

My Mom essentially retired from working in a skilled nursing home. Being raised around geriatrics, helping those who cannot help themselves, it has influenced me and my found journey. When I was introduced to feminist ideology, I learned that it is never acceptable to marginalize. I do not have to agree with you or your actions, but it is my job to meet you where you are. It is not my duty to judge you because of a substance abuse disease, mental health disorder, an intellectual/developmental disability, differences in sexual orientation/expression, different faiths or lack thereof, housing status, immigration status, education level, or any other personality or human difference that makes us unique. I sincerely value the fact that humans are unique. The most difficult clients I have to work with are those who are registered sex offenders (male or female) because their actions are not in line with my value systems, yet they are human and deserve compassion. Let me be clear. Being compassionate does not mean you excuse!

My hope is that you have read every chapter not because I wrote them but rather because they seriously build on concepts. Cherry-picking what you would read is not going to help because you will have become lost. I hope if I have rubbed you wrong, you know I am okay with that, value you, appreciate you, likely do not agree with you. However, I applaud that you want to make a difference in people's lives.

If these concepts are not new to you, maybe they are useful reminders. Maybe you are that Program Manager who needs a guide to help your newest staff member succeed. Regardless of why you started reading this, I hope it was meaningful and purposeful! These stories, as indicated in the introduction, are my clients' stories and their journeys with this social worker, geriatric provider, and now having been Legal Guardian to my late Father.

Seriously, my choice to be a feminist and identify as a born-again, a male, and an ally of the LBGTQ movement—these are my value systems. At no point in this book have I asked you to change your value systems. Perhaps something has caused you to question your dogmatic ways? That is good. We should question why we believe what we believe and be ready to defend it. That is the means of making our clients more empowered. If you have found that social service is what you want to do but you are still not certain what avenue, specialty, agency, or such, maybe this is your start. Most of all, my expected mandate for all social workers is to be compassionate!

Conclusion

My life has truly been blessed by amazing circumstances that changed me and my life's direction. I have lived through a very negative romantic relationship that allowed me to appreciate my wife. I have experienced pain, sorrow, trauma, and amazing adventures. My own life trauma, ACEs, affirmations of faith (and betrayals by faith community), coaches, teachers (academic and Sunday School), and bosses who invested in me, my journey remaining sober, being homeless, and my mental health break have made me the social worker I am today.

When I write about the impact of housing, compassion, recovery from substance abuse and alcohol, struggles with mental health, and searching for meaning, these are not just because my clients have lived these struggles; I, too, have lived it. I want to publicly thank Roger Fogg, FNP, for answering my after-hour crisis calls and saying that he would see me the next morning. That office visit, the medication he started me on saved my life. I want to thank my best friend in college for being a listening ear and disclosing to me honestly when I asked, "How long would you have let me remain in that state before you had acted on behalf?" And she replied, "You had until the weekend to get help, or I was going to get you help." And I know she would have. Seriously, getting your clients committed for mental health may not seem like the best thing, but if they, unlike myself, are not strong enough to seek their own help, it may be their funeral instead you will be attending!

It was an unofficial Holiday; I was loading the car to go to my family's house for a BBQ and received an instant message on social media from a family member. They were in an immediate crisis and needed urgent medical care, likely alcohol and drug care as well. I asked, "What is your phone number and address?" I learned that this person had their phone stolen and had been beaten up. I asked if I could call one of their immediate family members, and they said no but wanted their parents notified. This person did not know if their Mom and Dad would accept the call. The Mom answered the phone. I explained the problem, and she said the Dad was at the church. I sent the Dad a text message in ALL CAPS to ensure he understood the urgency. I asked this person if I could call an ambulance without law enforcement. Some time went by, but I did not get a response. Because of my credentials, I am obligated to get someone help when aware. I called that area's Crisis Department, but they could not help. I decided against calling 911 for that area because that will surely send law enforcement. Instead, that city's ambulance is privatized; therefore, I called the ambulance company directly and gave the address that was given.

I had asked the ambulance company not to call law enforcement as this would only complicate the person's problem. I read to them the instant message to state how badly this person needed a hospital. Sadly, the ambulance company did dispatch law enforcement instead of waiting to determine if it would be needed. This caused resentment between this person and their impression of what I did until I was able to establish a phone conversation confirming this person was in their Dad's care on the way to the hospital. I expressed what I did, why I did it, and what I advocated and that my advocacy was not respected. This person said they trusted I did what I said I did. I expressed that with my certification, I am required to ensure I get help within my scope for someone in crisis like this. I asked them to ensure they reach out to me again if they end up in crisis and to understand I will do what is necessary to meet their needs. I write this to explain that sometimes, getting your clients and/or family help is not what they want; however, we are not granted that choice; we are trained to meet a specific need within our training and must act on our training. Your training is not just applied to people you are paid to support; it is a 24/7 responsibility.

Before my mental health break, I had become homeless and had to humble myself to ask my mother-in-law if I could move in with them and my girlfriend (who became my wife) because the roommates I had helped had ruined my housing. Fast-forward, I had become homeless (for the second time) as a young married man with my wife and our newborn, and it was my mother-in-law and her wife's compassion that bought a travel trailer to put on their property for us to live. That was two years of living in a travel trailer before we could get into our own place. The landlord who rented to my wife and I and our two-year-old changed our lives and gave me an appreciation for a landlord who will grant my clients a chance.

I know the struggle of going from making a good salary to a minimum wage all because I am driven to support my family and defend my integrity. In a foster home, I was the Resident Manager, and the provider called me in the office and said, "I will give you your two days off and a raise if you agree to move your wife and child out." I told her, "You can keep your raise, and in thirty days, I will be moving and finding another job." And I did. That action cost me a good salary and my housing, yet my belief in my family was greater than my salary.

When people say, "But you have a college education," let me first say, "I never went to college to impress anyone." And college should help you become a more rounded person. My life could be any one of these stories, and if it was not for the kind and compassionate people in my life, I would not be where I am. In fact, I am convinced I would likely have died if Roger Fogg did not tell me, "I will see you tomorrow at eight a.m." When I went back to school to get my Master's in Business Administration, it was because I was underemployed, and my undergraduate education did not give me a strong enough understanding of business (my own choices of courses is not a failure of the university system). And that drove me to return to school. My first time attending college was in person, my MBA was online, and I believe that has helped me navigate clients who want to consider school.

Part of my Women's Studies experiences was my "Liberation Act," and my "Liberation Act" happened in part because I took another class's assignment too seriously and my Mom came to visit. In my Interpersonal Communication class, the professor asked us to write an outline of significant events and people in our lives; it was thirty pages later I turned in the assignment. My Mom had come to visit, and she had asked if she could read it. I told her, "I take no responsibility of how you feel. If you are hurt, it is my life and how I saw it." And the act of my mother reading my outline created a relationship that had been fragmented by my moving in with my Grandparents. My college professor approved me sharing the outline and the experiences that followed as my "Liberation Act," and I hope if you are wanting to have a "Liberation Act" that maybe the act of doing selfless social services for people who can never repay you may be your start.

As I have explained in this book, the faith I was raised with is not the faith I ascribe. My parents' choices of faith are not mine. I support their faith to the degrees possible, yet I am true to my God and the worship of my God. I was raised in a Republican home (there is nothing wrong with that or any other political party), became a Democrat once I registered, and left the Democratic Party to become what I am today—an Independent Party member. In many respects, my journey of finding love, acceptance, and my passion for social services is because I am a freethinker.

This book is dedicated to three special people: my high school coach and boss, the late Michael DeRobertis; my professor, the Women's Studies Program Chair who embraced a man who identifies as a feminist, the late Dr. Barbara Scott-Winker; and my beloved coworker and fellow Social Services Director who lost life's battle to cancer, the late Pamela Sanchez. Sincerely, these three people—a coach, an academic mentor, and a coworker—influenced my life. In case you were wondering, it was Pamela Sanchez who preached, "Cover Your Ass." And if you take nothing away from this book, in social work, life, and careers, you must look out for yourself by "covering your ass." And like the late Coach DeRobertis challenged me, "Either you're going to be coachable or I am not going to coach you." I want to thank Beth Plater for designing my cover and Barbara Fahn for lovingly caring for my Father when others would have given up. I want to highlight that my work as comprehensive social worker has been applied to my cousin, her Mom, and other family as her

Dad, Freddy Gardner, had passed. When you read these pages, these stories, the dedications, and the convictions of faith and training are personal and true. Nothing written in this book is fictional. Neglect happens; hospice and death happens. However, social workers can also be part of empowering and rewiring our clients. I want to thank my wife for standing by me and believing in me and my children for teaching me how to be a better social worker.

In case you are wondering, the chapters that I have loved writing the most are "My Client Smells" and "How to Interview for a Social Worker Position" because these chapters have affected how I engage with my clients and how I have interviewed. And now I want you challenge you. What stories of your life journey or clients' journeys can you tell? I thought I had concluded this book, and then COVID-19 hit. That caused me to write an additional chapter that I must also admit was fun to write because it demonstrates that social work is never the same, that it requires being comfortable with change. In fact, if we as social workers cannot adapt to change, we cannot believe our clients will accept change—let that sink in!

I sincerely want to thank my wife, Kristine Eldridge, for believing in me and my three boys, Zyler, Michah, and Geoffrey, for understanding that being a social worker means investing in others, as I could never have accomplished the journeys with my Dad, Grandma, or others without my wife and children being part of that journey.

I want to thank everyone who has taken time to read this printed copy, those who listened to me on the phone as I prepared to finish this, and those who volunteered to edit and provide feedback. This book would never have become published had it not been for the strong encouragement of my Speech and Debate friends and mentors, Jan and Lynn Pizzo. My Mother, Dena Eldridge, instilled, along with her ex-husband / my late Father, Jack Eldridge, values and principles that have guided my work and journey in social work. There are too many to list and some who would not want public recognition. Although this book is not dedicated, I want to thank Mrs. Kristi SanRomani, my high school Speech and Debate Coach, for believing in me, coaching me, and helping me become a better-rounded person, thinker, researcher/nerd. Her contributions, like Mr. DeRobertis, my paternal Grandparents, Russell and Carol Eldridge, who moved me into their home, and my in-laws who provided compassion and housing, will never be forgotten. Jack D. Eldridge, my Father, a man I proudly helped manage his care, may you find rest with your heavenly Father joined with your Mom, my Grandma, whom I shared the responsibilities of managing care and estate.

Glossary of Frequently Used Industry Terms

ACEs : Adverse Childhood Experiences. These are traumas from our childhood that can affect us as adults or how we engage in life events and circumstances—a very simplistic definition.

A&D: Alcohol and Drug Treatment. This can also include gambling for those who needs this help.

ADLs: Activities of Daily Living. These are specific tasks that a client/patient can do or needs to do and tasks that are assisted and/or identified as being deficient and/or successful.

Assisted-Living Facility: This can be an ALF or Residential Care Facility (RCF). It is licensed by the State to provide geriatric care, with coordination of an RN and an Administrator.

Assume: The act of making "an ass out of you and me" as outlined by Mr. Manley in ninth-grade social studies block.

Biases: Anything that creates your own paradigm that may affect how you judge or treat your client. These are natural but should not be used against your clients.

CADC: Certified Alcohol and Drug Counselor. This is anyone who has completed their education requirements and passed the exam to gain certification.

Care Plan: This is the formal document that details the plan of care this client/patient will receive, who provides it, what the client/patient does, and is the document that guides care.

CCO: Coordinated Care Organization in Oregon that (at the time of this publication) manages the client's Medicaid Benefit.

Dual Diagnosis: This is a client who has both a mental health and A&D issue needing cooperative treatment; it can also include gambling and mental health if A&D is absent.

Foster Home: A licensed home by an official regulatory office that is inspected and relicensed annually to provide managed care for clients. Licenses mandate acceptable level of treatment.

Golden Thread: The means of capturing the task, the goal, and the interaction and how it relates back to the Treatment Plan, Care Plan, and/or Service Plan. Documented cause/effect.

LBGTQ: Lesbian, Bisexual, Gay, Transsexual/Transgender, and Queer. It is a movement, and it is an identity, but not everyone who is part of this identity is part of the movement.

LMP: Licensed Medical Pactitioner. This is anyone with an advanced medical degree above a Registered Nurse status—Nurse Practitioner, Physician Assistant, and/or Doctor.

Memory Care: In Oregon, these institutions are specifically licensed for those with documented dementia and/or Alzheimer's Disease. They are not open to anyone like Assisted Livings.

Peer Mentor: In A&D, they are Certified to work with CADC to mentor clients through shared experiences. In Mental Health, they are peers who are in recovery with their mental health.

PCI: This is Pre-Commitment Investigator associated (in Oregon) with the County of client record who makes legal recommendations to the Court to hold client/patient in hospital.

PCP: Primary Care Physician. Nurse Practitioner, Physician Assistant, and/or Doctor who works in connection with medical assistants, LPNs/RNs to meet patient medical needs.

PHI: Personal Health Information. It can be anything that identifies a client by name or status with an organization. It is likely to change as technology advances. Be ready to adapt to it.

QMHA: Qualified Mental Health Associate. In Oregon, we are not Certified, and this is gained through education and/or specific experience with the SPMI population.

QMHP: Qualified Mental Health Professional. This in Oregon is now Certified and is a person with a Master's degree in a clinical field, including Social Work, Counseling, Psychology, etc.

ROI: Release of Information is your key to gaining PHI that cannot be disclosed without consent.

Service Plan: This identifies the number of hours a client receives, what their care needs are, how best to meet them, and their demographics and helps guide the PSW's interaction(s).

SNF: Skilled Nursing Facility. These are licensed treatment facilities with 24/7 nursing and nursing assistant staff providing care in accordance with doctors' orders. Some are also long-term care.

SPMI: Severe and Persistent Mental Illness. This is used to identify a client/patient who has a major mental health diagnosis that affects their ability to coexist.

Trauma: This can be actual and/or perceived abuses, neglect, or grievances in life.

Treatment Plan: This is the document especially in mental health that guides the client/patient care and what objectives are ascribed for them, and the Golden Thread is established through this.

Transitional Housing: This is any housing that is not intended to be long-term, maybe has independent skills training, or is specific in scope of time allowed to stay (i.e., six months).

UA: Urine Analysis. This screens for the presence of drugs and/or alcohol.

Wrap Around Services: Traditionally, Wrap Around is a child team concept. This book refers to it as any other service provider who can be coordinated through your efforts to meet clients' needs.

About the Author

This book was written because Matthew A. Eldridge's education did not qualify him for social work, geriatrics, or necessarily coaching. Instead, what qualified him was his compassion, life circumstances, and parenting, advocating for his late paternal Grandma and Father, who died with dignity on hospice but as result of negligence by the mental health facility, who Dad's care was entrusted.

Matthew's faith, values, and interpretation of faith are his; he has no belief his audience will share the same. He expressed some controversial ideas in this book, and he only asks for an open mind and for the reader to feel free to disagree. If people are all in the business of meeting people's needs, that is what matters.

Matthew, at the time this book started, before publishing, has made a career in geriatrics, including foster home, in-home caregiving, and in-home caregiver agency management, was a Certified Qualified Mental Health Associate (QMHA) in the state of Oregon, USA, has been in alcohol recovery since 2005, has a mental health diagnosis (Bi-Polar I), tobacco disorder in remission, and alcohol disorder in remission, and is happily married with three boys. He has worked in nearly all fields of health care, outpatient treatment for alcohol and drug, and mental health and has been a successful high school Speech and Debate Coach and pediatric and adults with developmental/intellectual disabilities support worker and/or foster care provider. He completed two undergraduate degrees and a minor. Years later returning to graduate school, he earned his Master's in Business Administration (MBA), graduating with honors.

This is not meant to be an academic book where the academia may get something useful; rather, it is meant to empower each reader to gain skills or sharpen skills that will impact the lives they encounter. Matthew welcomes the reader to come join these real-life journeys.

Please feel free to follow and/or connect on LinkedIn and share in the journey of impacting those who may never be able to repay.